COMPASSION FOR THE HUMAN CONDITION

COMPASSION FOR THE HUMAN CONDITION

Gurdjieff Meetings with Dr. and Mrs. Welch in New York

Selected Transcripts 1991–1997

DR. WILLIAM J. WELCH
LOUISE M. WELCH

Epigraph Books
Rhinebeck, New York

Compassion for the Human Condition: Gurdjieff Meetings with Dr. and Mrs. Welch in New York © 2018 Peter Kahan

Photograph of Mrs. Welch courtesy of Martha Henrickson

Paperback ISBN: 978-1-944037-90-1
Hardcover ISBN: 978-1-948796-03-3
Library of Congress Control Number: 2018930222

Book design by Colin Rolfe

Epigraph Books
22 East Market Street, Suite 304
Rhinebeck, New York 12572
(845) 876-4861
EpigraphPS.com

PREFACE

B EGINNING IN THE FALL OF 1985, until Dr. Welch's death in the summer of 1997, the meetings of what was informally known as the "Friday group" were recorded on cassette tapes. This was with the knowledge and encouragement of Dr. and Mrs. Welch. The hope was that, at some point, these recordings would be useful for those who had attended the meetings and perhaps also for others.

It goes without saying that we found the Welches' particular way of transmitting Gurdjieff's teaching both helpful and touching. The pupils of Gurdjieff who continued the teaching after Gurdjieff died each had their own emphasis, their own somewhat personal ways of transmitting their understanding of the objective truths brought by Gurdjieff. For those who were brought up in one particular lineage of the Work, it can now be very helpful to be exposed to other approaches. We hope the selections in this volume will help both those who have been engaged by the Work ideas for many years and those who are just starting out on their journey.

In the early 1970s, some of us, who were quite young in the Work at that time, began to hear about one of Mrs. Welch's major questions regarding transmission of the essential teaching of Gurdjieff: could the process take place without invoking fear in those trying to study and understand the teaching? Gurdjieff, as one pupil so aptly stated, could "knock you over, but catch you before you hit the ground." But when some of his pupils tried to copy his methods after he died, the results were not always so good and, indeed, on rare occasions, quite harmful.

The period from which these selections were taken, from 1991 until just before Dr. Welch's death, was a difficult time for

Dr. Welch. Mrs. Welch was afflicted with a progressive form of mental decline, which began to affect her in the early 1990s. As a result, Dr. Welch gradually took on the leadership role for their groups.

The extent to which Mrs. Welch was able to participate in the meetings varied a great deal. Sometimes she was, indeed, as sharp and insightful as she had been years before, but at other times she had to rely on Dr. Welch to respond to our observations and questions.

It was very interesting to us that, although Mrs. Welch became progressively less able to speak in the way she had before, the disease only affected her mind and her language abilities. Emotionally she continued to have the same strength and sensitivity as always. And often, as a meeting progressed, she would once again be able to speak coherently and with great insight.

With so much material in recorded form, there was the question of what material to transcribe, and then what to use in the present text. Since the transcribing of tapes was done over a period of many years, in fits and starts, there was a certain amount of randomness in the choices. Nevertheless, there is a reasonable variety in what has been selected and a good representation of the Welches' way of seeing the world and the Gurdjieff teaching.

In order for the reader to hear Dr. and Mrs. Welch's actual voices, four audio selections are available to those who have purchased this book. You will find them at this web site: *welch. whaleylakehomepress.com.* In these selections, the question, or an explanation of the question, has been dubbed in, instead of the voice of the original speaker.

Dr. William J. Welch and Mrs. Louise M. Welch met in 1934. Mrs. Welch had been part of A. R. Orage's Gurdjieff group in New York City since the late 1920s and Dr. Welch, in the midst of a career change from advertising to medicine, joined the Work soon after they met. They married in 1941.

Mrs. Welch had met Gurdjieff when he came to New York a number of times in the decade before World War II, but Dr. Welch did not meet him until he returned to New York after the war in 1948. During that time, the Welches were among the participants in his daily activities. Summoned to Paris by Gurdjieff, Dr. Welch was the attending physician during Gurdjieff's last illness in October 1949.

Dr. and Mrs. Welch were part of a small group of Gurdjieff's followers in New York who carried on his teaching after he died. This group established the Gurdjieff Foundation of New York in 1953, and it continues to this day. Dr. Welch was the president of the Foundation from 1984 until his death in 1997. In addition to working with groups in New York, the Welches worked with groups in Toronto and Halifax, and, on occasion, with groups in Europe.

Their own books are highly recommended.[1] There is additional material at www.gurdjieff.org/welchdr.htm and www.gurdjieff.org/welch.htm.

---

1   Mrs. Welch's book *Orage with Gurdjieff in America*, Routledge & Kegan Paul, 1982, gives an account of the Work in New York during the time Mrs. Welch was in Orage's group. Dr. Welch's autobiographical book *What Happened In Between: A Doctor's Story*, Braziller, New York, 1972, devotes several chapters to Gurdjieff, including the events surrounding his death.

TABLE OF CONTENTS

JANUARY 11, 1991

"Nothing has changed." Being available to the light of consciousness

First Questioner:

I was looking in my journal from 1980. I was surprised and somewhat stunned, I think, by the fact that the same things that concerned me then concern me now, and yet I think now that they are new. They are what you would call—if you were feeling critical—petty things, but certainly everyday things: the wish to be organized, the wish not to be negative, the wish not to consider so much, and so on. I think what I feel is that I'm too caught up in the content of what goes on, instead of trying to see more who I am. I'm really taken with that. I really think I can become a better person, so to speak, though not quite so overtly. And until I saw this in the journals, I was certainly taken in by it. I thought it was new: "This year I really am going to be different." Then I saw that I had said the same thing ten years ago.

It seems close to the question of what I really want. You asked me in our first interview to try to sit quietly and ask that question, "What do you really want?" And an answer came, which wasn't from my head, but it was something that was a surprise to me, and it was just, simply, the realization of what I am. And yet when I ask myself, in ordinary circumstances, I can't find that. That really truly isn't what I want at that time. Rather, I want to be different, I suppose. I just feel I'm too personal, still, after all this time.

I don't understand as much as I would wish. I think that "What do I want?" is in that area. I wish to understand more.

Mrs. Welch:

I think that's a very interesting and important recognition, because from one point of view I can only understand in terms of *my* way of understanding. And at the same time, there is a wish to be impartial in a way that would take into account, let us say, the truth of what is going on. And yet we all have our particular way of responding to it, judging it, and so on. I think the hunger for true impartiality is real. And yet, I see, over the years, how I have certain tendencies that come from what I regard—whether I know it or not—as important, what really matters, and so on. It's not a judgment that takes everything into account, because I have a point of view that influences everything more than I realize. Now, how to know *that*, with a certain objectivity, is, I think, what you're reaching for. How is it possible to be more impartial and exact at the same time? Because one can't be afraid of facing some of those unpleasant truths that emerge.

Dr. Welch:

How can one understand? I think that looking in a journal is a very interesting experience: to see that nothing has changed. What can this tell one? We all ask the same question for fifty years, in one guise or another. But there is an inevitable involvement in what you were saying—in the contents rather than the way in which it's processed, if you like—because all this stuff is familiar, seductive, and continues to be magnetic, in a way. I don't say that to myself, but I see that it's so, that it takes me.

Same Person:

But it seems, from reading the journals, that it clearly goes nowhere. So what if I'm better organized than I was? I'm going to be organized just before I leave.

Dr. Welch:

Yeah, suppose you were better organized. What are you organizing?

Mrs. Welch:
And what difference does it really make?

Same Person:
Yes, that was the thing.

Mrs. Welch:
But to see that is already different from having imagination about it, because it allows room for more material to enter. Maybe one can see better and be more inclusive in what one has to take into account.

Dr. Welch:
I think that journals of this kind are fascinating. The husband of Virginia Woolf lived to be about eighty-nine, and he kept a journal. He was the founder of Hogarth Press. Everything they published on the Hogarth Press is still in print and selling.

Mrs. Welch:
And will be for a long time!

Dr. Welch:
I remember a marvelous account he gave of his concern when a young man, whom they brought in to help them with the press, wanted to enlarge it and increase its scope. And of his counter effort to make this young man see that this was not required, that they were polishing diamonds, not making tinsel.

He was an admirable fellow. He was a member of the inner council of the House of Commons and very effective in this role. And he supported and really contrived to keep Virginia Woolf on track during long periods of acute psychosis.

And at eighty-nine he said, "I cannot see that anything I've done, in the course of my life, has meant anything at all." That it was nothing. There was no real substance. That's when he made that nice remark that "It's the journey and not the destination." But what was touching, in a way, was that he came to a kind of final, not agitated, disenchantment with all the sound and fury of his life. And he was very much with his marbles at eighty-nine, very much.

But what does it mean, really—where we are—to contemplate the notion of "dying to like and dislike"? Because that's really what the death in life is about. It has to do with transcendence, with understanding, with becoming aware of the value of "yes" and "no."

You want to be organized rather than disorganized. What is the heart of order? It's *inner* order, really, an inner hierarchy. One always looks to the contents for a resolution, but the resolution transcends the contents.

So, it's impossible, in a sense, to measure the distance between where I am and where that is. And, maybe, one just settles for recognizing the extraordinary evidence of the repetition of the automaton and the absence of what is called conscious attention.

The possibility of being available to another energy frees one from fear, because it's really fear that is there.

I don't know that one can entertain ideas of easing the sorrows of His Endlessness, or how one can entertain ideas of being an effective transmitter of the energy that the earth needs. All this gets very hard to be really connected with, but one can see inner slavery and what the real cage is in which one turns. Or maybe it's like the squirrel... [mimics the sound of a tread-wheel in a cage]. It's a little appalling to see that even ten years ago you could have told your fortune. You can tell your fortune to the year 2000.

Same Person:
[laughing] Well, there are some things that I do think have changed. [general laughter]

Dr. Welch:
Well, I grant you that.

I think Eliot said that all you have to do is count the teacups, and you'll know how long you'll go. This is not a counsel of happy prospects. But one sees that today is what yesterday was. And you see it very vividly in looking at what you seriously recorded as the avenue of approach, and you look back and say, "Oh, no. After all this time?"

Mrs. Welch:
Don't you think that, in a certain way, the question "What shall I do?" disappears, and what takes its place is "What is the right direction?" There's a major difference between them.

Dr. Welch:
"How shall I be?"

Mrs. Welch:
Yes. And how can I find that place where the right decision is more possible?

Dr. Welch:
The way you put it is "Where to turn?" rather than "What to do?"

Same Person:
I guess, this morning when I was going to the Foundation, I realized that I don't feel anything. What I think I meant was that I don't feel good, or interested, or excited. I just was flat, but I went anyway. And the way it came to me, which may not be quite the same thing, is, "Well, what's possible? What really can I see?" I was doing something with my hands, and I just wanted to see how much I could see. I had a recurring thought in my head that kept taking me away, and then I would go back to what I was doing with my hands. But I felt I couldn't stop what was going on in my head. I felt on the verge of finding a way to just see it, but I didn't, and then it was much later. I don't have enough...

Dr. Welch:
Attention.

Same Person:
Attention. Yes, that's exactly what it is. At the same time, that's what I felt I wanted: just to see it. To a certain extent I did, because I still know what the silly thought was. And it occurred to me, "Isn't that odd, that you're thinking this in a little scene?" I was in a little scene with somebody, in my head. But it's actually completely meaningless, because it has never happened. It's just imagination, where one wins, you know, against somebody. But I was actually doing something else. If I hadn't been going backwards and forwards...

Mrs. Welch:
You might have missed it altogether.

Same Person:
Yes.

Mrs. Welch:
At least you had a certain clear vision, even though, a moment later, it gets mixed.

Dr. Welch:
Well, one wants to feel good.

Same Person:
But you do feel quite differently when there are other people there. That's the sort of amazing thing. It's nearly always the case that when you're working with other people, even though you don't have much energy yourself, you always do end up feeling lighter, freer.

Dr. Welch:
Yes. Does one see that?

Same Person:
You see it at the end of a cleaning, as much as I still resist to go.

And I always go now, but I always find myself feeling a little sick at six o'clock on that evening.

Dr. Welch:
"I really...ahhumm... I'm not sure I should turn up" [mimicking]

Same Person:
Right. I always feel as though I may be coming down with something. But now I know that, and I just go. Over the last few years, I always feel I have more energy at midnight than when I went in. And it's because of the people together, trying.

Dr. Welch:
What doesn't one understand about that? It's the difference between what I want and what I need, you know. It's not so easy to see the difference between what one wants and what one needs.

Same Person:
One's emotions are so sort of wrong, in a way. They're so off base sometimes.

Dr. Welch:
There is always resistance. And a great big struggle, because you've got a pattern set up so that you just can't not turn up. But, at least in retrospect, you see the value of the little struggle: "I won't even take my temperature; I'll just go." Why isn't it sufficiently persuasive to last until the next time? Because the next time the same thing goes on. And you have the experience of having put the instrument into honing, or whatever is done, whatever takes place, so that you can't not go. And then it turns out that your memory about it is retrospect and not very prolonged.

So, why not just give it all up?

Same Person:
You mean the Work?

Dr. Welch:
Yeah, the whole enterprise! Forget yourself.

Mrs. Welch:
In a certain way, yes.

Dr. Welch:
Why not forget yourself?

Same Person:
Well, I've sort of tried that.

Mrs. Welch:
Well, how about breathing afresh? I mean this is what is needed there, that the rhythm has to change.

Same Person:
But, I'm not really kidding. I have tried that, sort of, over a period of weeks, and said, "Well, I can, you know. I mean I'm not bound to this. I don't have to keep on with this."

Dr. Welch:
That's right. This is not the Communist Party.

Same Person:
What happens, after several weeks, is that questions start coming back, which, for me, can only be answered by participation in what I consider to be the Work. The questions that come up are always of that same nature: "What is it all really about? What is the meaning of being here?" Just living a sort of ordinary life doesn't seem to... I always end up with a dissatisfaction.

Dr. Welch:
People who have no connection with the Work have said this very well, in many ways: "The unattended life is not worth living." Well, what does that really mean, the unattended life?

Mrs. Welch:
It means the unaware life.

Dr. Welch:
Yes, it means that the unaware life leads to a curious dissatisfaction, and to that question: "What the hell is this about? What
is this treadmill?" And then one turns to the treadmill, and it
doesn't help. But one sees that there are levels in which one is less
trapped in the demanding inner life, with all the reflections of
what the life of man is actually composed of. And it isn't a happy
prospect; it isn't filled with immediate satisfaction.

Sometimes one sees the comedy, but mostly one struggles with
the tragedy. The human comedy, the human tragedy, which is it?

Gurdjieff used to make such a kind of cosmic joke about our
situation. Were you at the reading the other day? Gurdjieff was
talking about how Buddhism was misunderstood and misinter-
preted. And the great tendency to wiseacre twisted this so much
that finally people ended up staying in cells, which only had a little opening at the bottom through which to put in a piece of dead
bread and some warm water. And they stayed there becoming
"conscious" until they died, and then were replaced by somebody
else. It was a pretty devastating thing, but he did it all with this
deadpan description of the results of wiseacreing. And it's only
funny if it's somebody else. It's not funny if it's you and me.

Mrs. Welch:
Well, the thing that is essential in undertaking anything is the
question of awareness of it. Because we undertake it, and then
the body gets into motion, let's say, and we get caught in that.

Dr. Welch:
We're no longer in two worlds; we're in one.

Mrs. Welch:
Yes. At least, we're in some variation of hell. The difference is being aware of it.

Dr. Welch:
We take our efforts very personally, and we think it is a bore and a waste of time and, "God damn it. What am I doing?" And so we drop it and then later say, "What did I drop?"

It's very hard to give leave of the idea that one is going to be other than oneself. Because one's self doesn't have to change. Anybody who assumes a new persona has dropped the ball. A new persona is not necessary. Personas are all equal, if you like. What one has, another one doesn't. And what one doesn't have, another one has. The idea is to allow the persona to continue to manifest as it does, but not without the light of what we call consciousness.

If there's the energy of the earth in man, and the possibility of the energy of heaven, if you like, and they're both there together, then that's fine. Otherwise it just spins down. And God knows, one looks around at one's seniors, and one sees that life has a way of spinning itself out quite predictably. It's no joke. "It's not for sissies."

Same Person:
The one question that comes, from what you said about not having to change, is what is it then that happens. Say you're in a Work situation, and, I guess you might say, you're in a somewhat different state, and you don't have the same fear or hesitation. I've mentioned this before. Sometimes in the kitchen at the Foundation, when someone asks a question, I know the way to answer it, and it seems right. It seems appropriate. It isn't coming from considering, or fear, or a wish to impress. It's just sort of appropriate. That's a change.

Dr. Welch:
You bet it is.

But it's not a permanent change.

Same Person:
Something comes through you, almost.

Dr. Welch:
That's right. Something comes through you. And that's what we're talking about.

Same Person:
And then you're the same old person the next day?

Dr. Welch:
Yes, the change is temporary, because the change is another inner order that isn't crystallized, if you like. It isn't set. It's a reshuffle. You know, I don't know whether we've said this a thousand times here, but it's clear that there is an order in oneself that can appear, quite without one's effort, in which violence is not possible.

Let's say Mme de Salzmann is here and she pumps you up. She really pumps you up, until you're in a place in yourself where you are not lost in junk. Junk doesn't interest you. You're suddenly alive to: "Even for me there may be hope. Even for me." There is hope here. And that doesn't last. But for the moment the water is wine. And then the wine becomes water again, when she's not there.

Mrs. Welch:
It just doesn't last very long.

Dr. Welch:
It just doesn't last very long. But, the reordering is what one is talking about. That's where one makes sense of this. The hypnotic state is changed, and one wakes up for a period.

The same thing can happen in other circumstances in which we don't necessarily understand the mechanism. In the presence of the real manifestation of nature—under the stars, let's say— one can be in a state in which the idea of violence can't appear. You don't begin to take in the scale of the universe, and at the same time, think about screwing somebody out of something, or suffering for some puny, personal abrasion of the ego. It is another level of being in oneself, and one is restructured, reoriented.

Mrs. Welch:
Alas, temporarily.

Dr. Welch:
Yes, it's temporary. But this work is about this sort of reordering, about trying to find the conditions that make reordering possible, the conditions that make one available to another quality of consciousness, another capacity for attention. And it isn't on the level of an angel. It has nothing to do with being an angel. It has to do with being—if you'll forgive the expression—a man. And I mean all cleft and crested.

But, you know, it's a change that is not inconsistent with the elements that reorganize themselves. And it begins with another state of the body, which is uptight; with another state of the head, which is separated; and with another state of the emotions, which are those of an uneducated horse. Nobody thinks that change is guaranteed. Nor—as we insist on imagining—is it necessarily something that I can arrange by tightening this, loosening that, shaving this down, or even just getting a catnap.

But, how does one remember this, with the elaborate machinery of the Foundation, and their work, and the committees, and the details, and the house on your back—busy with the Work, busy with the Work?

Mrs. Welch:
They are all meant to be a reminder, no?

Dr. Welch:
Don't misunderstand me. I can make a great case for it. But that isn't where my understanding is, necessarily.

Mrs. Welch:
We need it desperately though, don't we?

Dr. Welch:
Well, we persist in believing that the work is a linear pursuit of an

accomplishment. It's very hard. I don't mean that we can't formulate an elaborate account of how it isn't, but...

Mrs. Welch:
You know, when it's put into the terms, for instance, in which I first heard it, a century ago: "Be aware of your behavior, of your manifestation, at the time of its occurrence." And yet we all have the attacks of remorse about how we behaved, and so forth. But to replace that with the determination to be present to what takes place...

Dr. Welch:
And not to yield to the temptation to correct it, to judge it, to weep over it, to massage myself because it was so elegant—all the things that we do, except see it as clearly as we see it in other people. But even feeling as one does when one sees a little child manifest something that is evidence that they too are now in a trap. Well, you know, when you see them imitate you, doesn't it kill you?

Mrs. Welch:
Sometimes.

Dr. Welch:
But you don't criticize them, and you don't say, "You ought to be different." You say, "Oh, my God. Poor thing. There it goes." Isn't it so? [Several people objected that they do react when their own children behave outrageously.]

Of course we criticize them, if it's your own kid, and you're being exposed as a half-assed mother or a ding-dong father. But it isn't what I mean about the moment when you see the contrived behavior of something that is imitated and is rooted in some wonderfully budding little ego. It's touching; it isn't something else.

My favorite place for such things used to be the top of the double-decker buses on Fifth Avenue. Because when you're riding along, especially on an open one, you see people behaving in the street, and sometimes you see little children having a confrontation. I just happen to remember this one time very vividly. And it touched me deeply because it was such a parody of human behavior. And they were too little to be a threat. I just thought, "Oh, my God, look at this." It was a mirror of human absurdity.

It's not something that one can feel anything about, except what it means to "weep for the sins of Jerusalem." That's really what it is. One *sees* the helplessness of the puppets that we are.

Second Questioner:
How can you *not* want to change?

Dr. Welch:
Yes, how can you not want to change?

Same Person:
The more you say it, the more I don't believe it.

Dr. Welch:
No, I don't say that one doesn't want to change, but one has to see what change is. Change is being under another influence, being under the influence of your own higher mind. And it isn't "your own," but it's the connection with consciousness.

And of course it's difficult. Why? I don't know. Kundabuffer. That's my original sin. That's the analogy of original sin: "the, for them, maleficent consequences of the properties of the organ kundabuffer."

Third Questioner:
Well, is there the possibility for the development of our higher mind?

Dr. Welch:
You don't have to develop your higher mind. It's there, according to the theology of the Work.

Mrs. Welch:
But you're not always connected to it.

Dr. Welch:
What we're talking about is finding the inner conditions in which the organism is available to the light of consciousness. And this is *not* your best rational solution, nor is it something angelic. It is putting a driver in the front seat who can see and hear and knows what *is*, not what my "scenario producer" imagines is going on.

First Questioner:
For me, something hasn't been quite right in my work for quite a while. I don't know exactly what it is, but, earlier in the week, when I was asking a question in another group about obedience, something struck me, and a whole host of ideas suddenly became clear. It somehow cleared the air and made my situation less ambiguous than before. What became clear to me was that I had been relying on a form, and an idea, and a sense of what I was trying to do. And at that moment I recognized that I didn't have that form, that it was missing.

And at the same time, it became clear to me what was missing. In a simple way I saw that I had been relying on the presence of Mme de Salzmann, and that the clarity about what was required had been gone for a long time. [Mme de Salzmann had died about nine months earlier.]

Dr. Welch:
Do you know what she said about this? In talking to somebody she said, "In the presence of a teacher, the water becomes wine. Away from the teacher even your wine is flat." It's a very interesting thing to recognize, because it's true that something is crystal clear in the presence of... She didn't say, "In my presence." She was talking about something else. But one has this experience.

Same Person:
In her presence, the form, and somehow the content, was so palpable.

Mrs. Welch:

But that you are relating it to obedience is very interesting. Is that a question of attention?

Same Person:

Yes. But at the same time, what struck me was that I didn't have that inner obedience to want or to need to have that contact. It was clear that that was missing at that moment. And I think that it raises the question of what, in a sense, I listen to. Mme de Salzmann's presence was, for me, outer—a sort of ideal. It was not from the recognition of myself, but from the recognition of what is possible.

Mrs. Welch:

And how to be in touch with that when, let's say, she's not physically in this room? But there's something that is deeply related to it that *is* in this room. It's related in some very profound way to the whole question of being.

Same Person:

Can one ever reach the age of responsibility? That was the question that somehow came to me.

Dr. Welch:

Maybe. Perhaps. Sometimes.

Those were the three words that Gurdjieff always said were necessary if you wanted to speak English. [laughing] They answer almost all questions.

Mrs. Welch:

How can one understand the statement "I am"? And when it is answered with "I am that I am,"[1] one feels something about the statement. But how to understand it in depth? How to be available for it?

1   Exodus 3:14 "And God said unto Moses, I AM THAT I AM: and he said, Thus shalt thou say unto the children of Israel, I AM hath sent me unto you."

I think we're very much in search of that vibration, and there are times when we are much closer to it. There are times when we feel it, experience it, but it's still very much in process. Sometimes I'm available, and sometimes I'm not available, and part of my study has to do with recognizing the differences. I think you're touching something very essential there. And it's not something that I can do, in the ordinary sense of the word. How can I be genuinely available, genuinely receptive?

Second Questioner:
Does "being available" mean being more present?

Mrs. Welch:
That certainly must be a very powerful aspect of it, because unless the whole of me, in that sense, is present, how can I be, so to speak, reliable?

Dr. Welch:
What is not being available? Do you know when you're not available?

Same Person:
Well, I've experienced it and observed what it is.

Dr. Welch:
And what is it characterized by?

Same Person:
Well, what seems to take place for me is considering. For example, when I attempt to perform something, there is a difference between having my attention on my body, and not having that attention because I'm occupied with concern about whether or not I'm being well received. And the difference in the quality of the performance is that one is alive and one is dead.

Dr. Welch:

What does it mean to be closed? Because what we're talking about is being open.

Mrs. Welch:

This is a difficult question.

Same Person:

Again, it's sensory. There's no contact with the body.

Dr. Welch:

There may be contact with the body, you know. But what is the state of the body?

Same Person:

I would say that the body is tense and occupied with that.

Dr. Welch:

Pre-occupied. Taken by the head. Up tight in the body. Preoccupied and having its own agenda. Without *you*.

Same Person:

Oh, boy. It seems to me it's like containing a wild man.

Dr. Welch:

Well, probably *not* containing a wild man.

And at the same time, one has to be careful about being critical of this, because this is not anything other than the natural state of reactivity that is going on as a result of an inner passivity and an outer activity. And what is missing is inner alertness. A loose cannon. It's a play of forces having its way. And what are those forces? The head and the heart and the body running amok.

Mrs. Welch:

I've been thinking lately of the way in which the first commandment is stated. It begins with "I." "I am the Lord thy God." "I," as if to put such emphasis on what is really meant by that way of referring to oneself, to one's essence: "I." We use it in so many ways. Heaven knows how many sins we are guilty of in the ways that we use it. But there's also something that is essential and belongs to every being with potentiality.

Same Person:
I have had a couple of experiences in Movements where there has been a more specific attention on my back than I am used to having. And I was curious about why my attention seemed more available, or stronger, while that awareness of my back was occurring. I realized that when I sit, I don't have that strong an awareness of the distinction between being in contact and not being in contact.

Mrs. Welch:
You're not so much in touch with the alternatives at such a moment. If *I* am not, what's taking place? Who am I? So often we feel self-inventive—we've done so many things ourselves, and so on. But the statement is that the root of "I" is divinity.

And then we have to face this task of becoming conscious, conscious of one's identity, of what is taking place in oneself. When you speak of the body, that's the way a great deal of what we feel and know is felt and known. This is the shape we take. It may not be the only shape we take, but it's a very important part of it.

What is the study of the self? What is self-study? We recognize people in bodily differences, including tone of voice, including the way people move and everything that relates to them. But these are all evidences of something interior, something inner. How well does one know one's inner life? Manifestations are a wonderful way of teaching us, and yet how well can we recognize and know them, and know what they're saying?

Third Questioner:
It seems simple and clear when you talk about being available or not. But after a day or two of having found a kind of connection, I weave a web of a kind of *mea culpa*, or something. It's as if this delusion, or the form that my sleep takes, is that I think, "Well, I no longer have this connection because I didn't work." I'm wondering whether it's really just a question of being much simpler about it, rather than projecting that there's something I don't have.

I'm not willing to pay the price of really making an effort to be in touch with something, so...

Dr. Welch:
What would you do?

Same Person:
Well, I think it's an effort of another magnitude.

Dr. Welch:
Yes, but what would that effort be?

Same Person:
Well, to suffer the way that I am. Or to be able to see the way that I am.

Dr. Welch:
Yes, but what is the *effort* to see?

Same Person:
What is the effort to see? Well, it's simply seeing, I guess.

Dr. Welch:
But we have to be clear about it. Because, if it's just simply seeing, what's the big undertaking? Why effort?

What is at the heart of it?

Same Person:
Well, the experiences that I have of making a connection...

Dr. Welch:
What effort do you make in order to make that connection?

Same Person:
I think, primarily, it is letting go.

Dr. Welch:
And that's an effort? Letting go of what?

Same Person:
I think that in its simplest form it is tension or...

Dr. Welch:
How do you let go of tension?

Same Person:
Well, that's the problem. I don't know.

Dr. Welch:
But what is your *effort*?

Same Person:
Well, sometimes I think it's facing discomfort and to keep returning with my attention, to...

Dr. Welch:
[interrupting] Oh, with your attention. Ohhhh.

Mrs. Welch:
Aha. Now we've reached the magic word.

Dr. Welch:
And where is your attention?

Mrs. Welch:
Where is your attention? Where is *my* attention? Where is *our* attention? That's all you need, you know.

Dr. Welch:
All you have to do is pay attention. What is the quality of your attention? What is the effort?

Same Person:
Well, is that the same as the substance that animates my attention?

Dr. Welch:
Ba, ba, ba, ba, ba... "The substance that animates my attention." [mimicking it] Come on.

Same Person:
OK, is that the same force...?

Dr. Welch:
The chemistry of consciousness. [laughter] Come on. Try again.

Mrs. Welch:
Well, it starts an inquiry. You're trying something. It's not just anything now.

Same Person:
I mean, the preoccupation steals that force.

Dr. Welch:
Where is your attention if you're preoccupied?

Same Person:
Well, it's all over the map.

Dr. Welch:
No, it's with your preoccupation, sir. That's where your attention

is—where *my* attention is. Attention is taken, isn't it? By everybody but me.

And suppose you have your attention, to what do you attend? Why do you want that attention to be available to you?

I think that it's not undesirable to try to be clear, because there's enough moonshine around to last us all for the rest of our lives. And what we want is the light of the sun—not reflected. So, it isn't necessary to find your formulation. It's necessary to stay where the question is, in order to come to your *own* clarity of what the undertaking is, what the enterprise is, what the worldview is, what you are doing here. You know?

What am I doing here? Besides being good. Sometimes. Feeling virtuous. Sometimes.

Fourth Questioner:
One evening last week, I found myself able to see, intermittently, quite a lot of what was going on in me. I wasn't trying not to think or to not do anything. I just let thoughts come. It was very striking how much I could see of the tremendous amount of activity that constantly goes on. Thoughts go zooming by, and every thought has an image and some words. And every time I move, there's a visual image somewhere—sort of in the background—of where my body is, of the parts that I don't actually see. When I reach for something, several decisions are being made, all very quickly, and one thing associates to another, and so on. It was very striking because it was so active, and because part of me could watch it without its activity diminishing very much. I didn't associate as freely as usual, or in the same way, but there was certainly plenty of stuff going on.

Mrs. Welch:
How did you watch it? Do you know?

Same Person:
That's what was most striking. It was intermittent, but much more concentrated than the usual glimpse from time to time. I've

tried this, to a lesser degree, a couple of times since, and it's clear how my attention, or something that can watch, is taken by one or another of these associations. These associations could go on without my being taken by them. I have no idea exactly how to come to that kind of separation, and it took me a while to settle into it. Clearly, I need both interest and some persistence. And, in this case, I wasn't with anybody, so the concerns of identification were less overwhelming.

Dr. Welch:
Is it fair to say that what was unique about this was that, despite being interrupted by associations, by considering, by tensions, and so on, you kept coming back to the same place, to the state of observing, whatever that state is? What interests me is that, however it pulsated, it came back to the same place for a longer time than usual. It had some persistence, some common line that was familiar each time you came back.

Same Person:
One of the things that's interesting to me is that, usually, I think that I have to stop those associations. But rather I have to separate from them in a certain way.

Dr. Welch:
And that ain't so easy. I think it is very interesting that you were interested and not tense about it. There was an engagement with the mechanism rather than with the contents.

Same Person:
And when I tried, on a couple of other occasions, I really only saw that it was not happening. What I could glimpse was that when the identification, or the engagement with considering, was too strong, it wasn't so easy to drop it. And also, it really is an effort to try to keep dropping the identification, even though the effort is not muscular.

Dr. Welch:
Yes. To keep coming back. It's almost as if they were somebody else's associations and meanderings and worryings, and so they were less demanding. But when they become demanding, it's not so simple, is it? It always has seemed to me that if one's emotional concerns are seen as life and death, then they are life and death. It's not so easy to find one's way to relative objectivity, to see the emotional concerns rather than to be lost in them.

Same Person:
It's also clear, at times like that, that this is really my only life...

Dr. Welch:
Yes, The only hope.

Same Person:
...and that there's no need for speculating about souls or anything else. It's clear that *this* is my real life, and that, in a sense, the rest of my life is a waste.

Dr. Welch:
You know, the popular notion of the stream of consciousness is the stream of free association. And what you're saying is that the real stream of consciousness is not the contents of all this rubbish, but rather the awareness of oneself and of the associations, and seeing that it's going on by itself. Somebody is *there*.

Mrs. Welch:
I wish we knew more, or knew a way of knowing more, about attention. This is what, in a way, we're primarily concerned with.

Dr. Welch:
And it's the real mystery.

Mrs. Welch:
Sometimes attention is called, for example, by a loud noise, and so

on. But what we're trying to do is to be more attentive to attention, to wake up to attention.

Maybe being aware of it takes place in us more than we even know. But what we usually call our thought is just a movement of association. When we say, "Well I was thinking about something," what was really happening was a picturing, or some sort of verbal association, that began to call on other associations. But the question is whether I'm aware of it or not. If not, it's a totally mechanical process.

Same Person:
It's interesting about the confusion of calling it the steam of consciousness, because it's only because of moments of awareness that anyone is aware of the stream of consciousness.

Dr. Welch:
It's the stream of dreams. And the stream of consciousness is very broken up. There are long pauses, but when one has the experience of trying to be less fragmented, less dispersed, less lost in this, it becomes a different experience. You are interested and concerned, and then you find yourself lost in a maze of some sort of a dream about something that has *taken* you. And then you come back; you're interested to come back. And the stream of consciousness may be a broken stream, but one keeps returning to it, and one has the experience of some kind of inner continuity.

. . . .

It seems to me that the process of thought, which never stops, which confronts me, which contains my data bank, and so on, is really not terribly different from other processes in the body that are quite independent of my direction or initiation. And I think it's true in the lungs, and it's true in the kidneys, and it's true in the liver, and it's true in the guts. There are fabulous mechanisms that undertake to take care of the whole *megillah* of running this impossibly complex factory. And the factory includes a head end, which among other things is set up to perform things that we call mentation and cognition and memory, and so on. But on my own, I can't invent a thought.

I think the same thing can be said about the appearance, and disappearance, and bubbling up of emotional states. They appear; they are independent of volition or intention. We cheer ourselves up, and we quiet ourselves down, and we do all sorts of things. But the fact is that the pot is boiling, whether we're identified with what's going on, or whether we're not. We're lost in it. It's the tyranny of the horse.

I think that there is a real question about the process of thought. I have read—and probably everybody here has read— what appears to be extraordinarily lucid, orderly thought: perhaps what we call the muse of poetry, or scripture, or extraordinary scientific formulations. My notion of it is that this kind of relationship with thought may require a capacity to attend to what is taking place, a great engagement of interest perhaps, perhaps touching another level in oneself. It requires an ability to discriminate among associations and to see fresh possibilities of rearrangement, because most great ideas are rearrangements of something that has already been deposited.

I don't know this at all, but it seems to me that it's very hard to account for, in any other way, this extraordinary capacity to relate and store impressions in the form of memory, and to retrieve them in wildly unpredictable ways. And this capacity of cerebral relays, whatever they are, is something that is quite independent and takes me by surprise.

Same Person:
It seems to me that whenever I have a real thought, or a realization, or understand something, that it's a little bit like what has been described in much more dramatic form by some scientists, and by Mozart, for instance. Apparently he could see his whole symphony all at once, in an instant. And then, thinking it through is really no different than writing it down. It's just a physical

thing, in a sense. The real realization is something of a different order and very mysterious.

Dr. Welch:

I think that one is talking about the nature of creativity. If one would accept for a moment that there are levels of being, changes of state, and that they're not entirely unavailable, that they take place, then creativity can be thought of as sort of a quantum leap. It's a movement to a whole new set of landmarks. It's a removal from the arrangement in which one is customarily placed to another set of conditions. We've talked about this before. Koestler studied this very well, and viewed scientific generalizations that occur, and things like poetic imagery and laughter, as all being a change in dimension. One sees this very clearly with laughter: there is a rearrangement of the factors that have been under consideration. The whole thing becomes insupportable and incongruent, and is the occasion for abrupt laughter.

Same Person:

I think that any real understanding is like this, and that we actually are moving between levels much more than we think.

Belief and skepticism. Approaching objective truth. Inner reordering and will.
"Man is in essence a passion..." "Where are all the grownups?"

First Questioner:

It seems to me that I believe everything, and it's an accident if it's right. The only times I've ever come close to not believing something are when I'm trying to not move—when I'm trying to sit. I don't see that there's any separation from belief at any other time. But if I believe, then I'm not working. I'm just convincing myself. When I actually come to a stop, maybe that's what's called work.

Dr. Welch:

I think that we don't begin to appreciate how, in an ordinary way, we are the victims of an inner attitude, an attitude that we don't know exists. We wouldn't say, "I have an attitude," but we can see that we already have a view of something in ourselves—a way of looking at things. I see what I believe, but it doesn't occur to me that I see it in *my* way. And if I really talked with somebody else, I'd be astounded, because they have quite another view—maybe absolutely black, maybe absolutely white, but very different. And I don't think we begin to realize how much we believe, when we are really talking about revelation.

You [addressing another person at the meeting] and I were talking the other night about death by thirds. And it was clear to you, and it was clear to me, as we talked about it, that you were trying to get everything in shape to believe—just like that. Do you remember?

That Person:
Oh, yes.

Dr. Welch:
And I think it's interesting that one says, "Oh, that's the way it is. I believe it," instead of hearing it. I don't think we begin to understand what the word "skepticism" means, because it isn't negative in its real sense. It's really open, with a question instead of a decision. Whereas we think of a skeptic as being a...

Mrs. Welch:
Non-believer?

Dr. Welch:
Yes, just a non-believer. Or with a negative belief in something else. But one can't pretend to be a true skeptic. A true skeptic is one who is present to the data, to the evidence, to the event, without requiring to be lost in belief, or turned off by disbelief. Does that make sense to you?

First Questioner:
I don't know as I'm ever going to know that.

Dr. Welch:
I agree.

Same Person:
It seems to me that the difference between how I am and anything that would make any sense is rather overwhelming.

But I can almost hear you say, "It's a fuller life, nonetheless."

Dr. Welch:
Where did you hear that one? You believe everything! [laughter]

You know what Gurdjieff says about this? Man, contemporary man, and man as he is, "man in quotation marks," will believe, as he puts it, "any old tale." He'll believe any old tale. All you have to do is repeat it enough.

Same Person:
I believed everything I heard.

Dr. Welch:
Is there a mindset that makes you convinced that the Work is great stuff? Does everybody in the Work have a mindset about this? Who are the people who speak about "the path"? How much of belief is faith?

I think one has to ask oneself this, and not from the point of view of "yes" and "no," but from the point of view of a real query. Because there's a difference. One begins to understand that there are different ways of knowing. One can know something in one's head, but one knows something that one has experienced very differently. Isn't that true?

My favorite example of this is that a woman obstetrician who's had a baby knows a lot more about obstetrics than a man obstetrician who will never have a baby. And the man and woman obstetrician are just the same until she's had a baby, and then she has another view, a larger dimension, another quality of experience. It's like a surgeon who's been operated on—a very different guy than the one who goes chop-chopping. I remember one of the greatest surgeons, I think, of my time, who had a little cyst on his back, and one day he was about to have it taken off. A strange thing happened: he had a bad cold that morning, and he just couldn't do it.

Mrs. Welch:
He had a whole series of excuses.

Dr. Welch:
Absolutely. And he's one of the great surgeons of the twentieth century.

Mrs. Welch:
He had to trust other people's surgery, however, not his own.

Dr. Welch:
But I think it's interesting to question what one is taken in by, when one doesn't realize one is taken in. How is it possible to *stay* with a question? It's very difficult—very difficult, because some things are very persuasive.

Same Person:
It seems to me I need something that I don't have in order to do that.

Mrs. Welch:
I think that's a very good observation. I think it's true for all of us.

Dr. Welch:
Gurdjieff used to say about *Beelzebub* that people who read it take everything literally that is meant figuratively, and everything figuratively that is meant to be flat out. As Ouspensky would say, "It could not be otherwise."

Mrs. Welch:
I think it's a discovery. When one begins to doubt this in oneself, then it makes it more possible to inquire further, even into one's own experience. Why do I believe everything that one person says and almost nothing from someone else? It has something to do with my feeling about their character, or their basic honesty, and so on. But I could be quite wrong about that. What is it? I think that's an interesting question that you bring, and that you're wondering about, because we can't just take everything that comes our way as God's truth.

Dr. Welch:
I think it's interesting to examine this question in all walks of life. You know, Einstein's special theory of relativity wasn't really ver-

ified until 1919. The fact is that he had an open mind right up until then. He absolutely was not lost in his triumph of generalization.

Mrs. Welch:
I never believed in his disbelief.

Dr. Welch:
You can't not respect the difference between Einstein and Freud.

Mrs. Welch:
I respect them both.

Dr. Welch:
Yes, but I'm now talking about what happens to belief and to falling in love with something that becomes an obsession. It's very difficult to know where one stands. And it's very comforting to be reassured: "Well, I've got the answer for that." We all want to hear answers, and we all want to be reassured.

Mrs. Welch:
And we all want to hear the truth. So, there you are.

Dr. Welch:
Well, I'm not so sure. The truth gets pretty hot sometimes.
There's the great theory that everybody wants to know the truth. Do you remember that poem that you wrote, the first line of which was "Tell me the truth. I want to know"? It was about somebody who said to you that they wanted to know the truth. They damn near killed you.

Mrs. Welch:
That's right.

Dr. Welch:
You had to barricade yourself, when you tried to tell the truth. The truth about us is not necessarily very comforting.

Mrs. Welch:
Or visible.

Dr. Welch:
I'm afraid it's all too visible.

Mrs. Welch:
No, I think aspects of it are. I don't think the whole truth is visible.

Dr. Welch:
And you mean something nice, and I mean something not nice. [laughing]

Mrs. Welch:
I think potentiality is great, and I think everybody who is interested in the Work is...

Dr. Welch:
...available for affirmation.

Mrs. Welch:
...has potentiality. Which is the truth of things, no matter how unpleasant. Or...

Dr. Welch:
Or at least they think they do.

Mrs. Welch:
No, I think they do. It's a combination of things. But I think it's true. There's a hunger to know how things really are, in addition to wishing to make a good impression, and so on. But there *is* a hunger for truth. Not just for comfort, but for truth.

Dr. Welch:
You know that Madame said, "I have great difficulty knowing what it is that I think. At least I think I do."

Mrs. Welch:
You mean it varies.

Second Questioner:
As I'm listening to this conversation, I'm trying to make some sense out of it.

Dr. Welch:
Hmm. It's not so easy. [laughter]

Same Person:
Well, I'm trying to sort out the things you are saying, and see if there's a scale to them. There's something there that interests me. I know precisely what we've been talking about, about believing any old thing. I have this feeling of...

Dr. Welch:
Credulity. Gullibility. Suggestibility.

Same Person:
No, I believe my life to be one thing, and it's like an attitude. It's like looking through a colored glass. And with just a shift somehow, I can see it as other than that. I don't really understand that there's a certain reality to my existence.

Dr. Welch:
Wait just a minute. What is being said is that I don't see *all* of reality. I see what I can see. I see white light. I don't see infrared, and I don't see ultraviolet. It doesn't make them invalid. They're there, but I don't see them. And the analogy holds for a great deal of how we are. I have some wonderful buffers that keep me from seeing the way I am. It's not so easy to see the way I am. And I may believe all kinds of things. But there is objective...

Mrs. Welch:
Truth?

Dr. Welch:

...truth. So I see what I can see through my peepholes. After all, I can't register certain vibrations. Certain wavelengths are not visible to me. It doesn't mean that they're not there; they are. And this is the difference between Newton and Einstein.

There is something that is outside, not just my ego. There's something I can see with the extensions of my measuring devices: my touch, my smell, my sight, and so on. That's reality. But that's *my* reality, that's not reality with a capital "R." Einstein is talking about the big spectrum out there that isn't available to my measuring devices. That's all. It isn't dragging in some bizarre or exotic thing. It's really the question of the elements of what we're talking about: what is in me, and what is not in me.

Same Person:

It seems as though sometimes I'm aware that there is a God. And sometimes that's even something I can believe in. But most of the time I'm very disconnected from that thought.

Mrs. Welch:

You're distant from it.

Same Person:

Distant from it. Yet there are things that I know in myself that I call real, which have a whole different character to them, and yet are also real. And this petty way that I live my life—what I believe in, my complaints, my voices, all the stuff that goes on—is the wrong way to look at it. Recently some things have happened that have made me see, in a flash, that if this rosy glass—actually, it's not rosy, but rather grim and pretty dirty—is pulled away for a second, then I can see something. And I remember that. I know that's there. Yet this other thing is also real for me. That's how I live my life. But what I don't see is the whole picture.

Mrs. Welch:

It's effective, but that isn't necessarily *real* for you. I think there's a distinction there that you are not making. Something that influences, or affects, or even is in charge of my behavior and reactions, isn't necessarily the truth. It is the way I've been conditioned from the time I was quite young. And yet there is a hunger in human beings for a way of knowing what is true, not just what appeals, so to speak, in terms of being pleasanter, or in terms of being more convincing. How do we approach objective truth? How do we approach the possibility of seeing what really *is*, not just what we would like, or what would please us, or what we're very much afraid must be true about us, and so on. In a way, this is what you're after.

Same Person:
It occurs to me that sometimes I see the laws of the universe at work. And at other times, I suppose, these laws are working on me. You have talked about being a slave.

Dr. Welch:
What is your experience of that? Don't just believe it. What is your experience of slavery, or do you have such experience?

I'm not suggesting that you are required to give me a catalog. I don't mean that at all. But our imagination about what we initiate, and how we live our lives, is open to very serious question. Not that we don't accumulate a great deal of evidence of manifestation, but where did all this manifestation come from? To a certain degree, I have to acknowledge that I've been programmed. My life follows a pattern that everybody else's life follows. How come? How come I'm driven to be like this, and to do this, and to do that? Interesting.

Same Person:
Part of it has to do with the times that we live in.

Dr. Welch:
The times that we live in... The more they change, the more they're the same.

Same Person:
One thing has to do with whatever our purpose is here on Earth: to feed the moon, or something else.

Dr. Welch:
It certainly is not *my* purpose. I do a lot of things, but I don't have any basis for imagining that it's my purpose. I have the impression that I do a great many things without resistance, in a way. And even if I resist, I do them. I have a great many characteristics and manifestations that are quite enigmatic, from my point of view. And in the end I fulfill the nitrogen cycle.

Mrs. Welch:
It's not the whole of your life, however. It's an aspect of it.

Dr. Welch:
Thank you. [laughing]

Third Questioner:
But I also have the experience, occasionally, of being available to a different impression that sometimes sits with me. I'm intermittently cognizant that something is going on that's very unusual, and, in a way, almost vital. And I have no say in the matter. But when it happens, the circumstances are such that my activity is not taking all of me.

Dr. Welch:
It doesn't change the fact that you live in a dying animal.

Same Person:
Not at all. It doesn't even necessarily allow me to act intentionally. But to the degree that I'm aware of it, it suggests that there's another mode of seeing.

Dr. Welch:
You've heard about that, have you?

Same Person:
I've felt that, not just heard about it.

Dr. Welch:
Are you sure you felt that before you heard about it?

Same Person:
Well, that's a good question. It may very well be that I heard about it first.

Dr. Welch:
We're talking about what was said at the start: one hears about it; one believes it.

Same Person:
But I also felt it, and that is not "believing any old thing," and it's not my imagination. It's not unfamiliar, because it's almost as if it's organic, in a way. And it's connected with people. It's not just connected with some idea that I've had. In fact, any ideas that may be transpiring have nothing to do with it. At best, it's always a question: "How is it that I'm like this, that I'm experiencing this?" And I wish to. So I may find myself hanging around these conditions and events for as long as I can tolerate it.

All the things that you say that we are, I can't agree with entirely.

Dr. Welch:
What are you speaking of now, for example?

Same Person:
Well, my impression is that your general tack, in dealing with our questions or our statements, is one of bringing us in front of "What is your experience? Why is it that you're not rigorous about what you're saying?" And I think that's valid. But I also have the almost simultaneous impression that's there something you're either intentionally avoiding, or...

Dr. Welch:
Who is intentional?

Same Person:
…it's just that you're not seeing it.

Mrs. Welch:
That could be. [much laughter] Now, I want to ask you something. How do you face the statement like this one made by the Work: "Man is in essence a passion for understanding the meaning and aim of existence"? When you hear a statement of that quality, what is the effect on you? It has nothing to do with little personal things, and yet it's the most personal thing in the world, because it has to do with your life.

Dr. Welch:
It's not "man in quotation marks," by the way.

Mrs. Welch:
It's man—mankind, if you wish to put it that way. But it's related to that primary question of why we're here: a passion for understanding the meaning and aim of existence. There is something there that strikes a certain note of inquiry: Why are we here? By the accident of sex? Well, where did that come from?

Dr. Welch:
Do the manifestations of mankind bear this statement out?

Mrs. Welch:
I think they do. Well, this is the origin of all the great religions.

Dr. Welch:
I'm talking about the life of man.

Mrs. Welch:
Well, which life are you speaking of?

Dr. Welch:
Here they are. Here it is.

Mrs. Welch:
And these people are here because they wish to understand.

Dr. Welch:
Every Friday.

Mrs. Welch:
Oh, come on. They're here more than just every Friday.

Dr. Welch:
I'm not criticizing them. I'm not talking about criticizing, and I'm not talking about this small group of really pre-flight candidates. [laughter]

Mrs. Welch:
Some of them are successful candidates.

Dr. Welch:
I'm talking about the manifest history: the behavior, the manifestations, the awful show that man puts on. It is certainly very difficult to relate this to anything but a great misinterpretation, if this is a real drive.

Mrs. Welch:
We can get into a wonderful debate, and someday perhaps...

Dr. Welch:
No, I don't want to debate. But I think one has to be kind of tough about this. Otherwise, you can dream that you're transcending the really very enclosed life of man as he is.

Mrs. Welch:
Nobody's recommending that. This Work certainly doesn't. But there is the question that everybody has: "Why are we here?"

Dr. Welch:
Sometimes.

Mrs. Welch:
Well, of course, sometimes. Most of the time we're just going about in our mechanical ways. But there is something at the heart of existence. Anybody with any kind of brain and any depth of feeling, anybody with substance, has these inner questions: "Who am I? Why are we here? What is man?" And all the great religions were founded in an effort to bring more material to this question. Wouldn't you agree with that?

Dr. Welch:
I agree with it, but I'm scared to death.

Mrs. Welch:
Well, that's good. That's part of it. Being scared to death is part of it.

Same Person:
It seems to me that although I can't initiate, being here often gives me the impetus to aspire, and so says something about what is potentially possible.

Dr. Welch:
Do you feel that I'm not crediting your testimonial?

Same Person:
No, quite the contrary. I think that I've undergone too many self-abnegations of the wrong variety, and I've undergone too many self-criticisms. And I fail to really see that, even for me, something is possible. There's so much of this *mea culpa* in my life, or there's just total blankness. Perhaps it's necessary for me to come here, or to circumstances like this, to just be reminded. I've tried experiments that have proven to me what you've said, over and over again: that I cannot do, even if I think I can do.

Dr. Welch:
What would "doing" be?

Same Person:
Well, keeping an appointment with myself at a regular time.

Dr. Welch:
Oh, that could be a compulsive habit.

Same Person:
I can't do it.

Dr. Welch:
Oh, yes you could. If you were nutty enough, you could.

Same Person:
Well, I'm not.

Dr. Welch:
No, but you can't reduce this enterprise to a discipline and being a trained automaton, a soldier, who is always on duty. One
is talking about another level of being, not criticizing the being
that we represent, not talking guilt, not talking *mea culpa*, but not
failing to recognize that one is talking about the difference between being an automaton or doing God's will. Now, this is really
not about getting to appointments on time. It can't be reduced to
something like eating plenty of fiber. That's the level on which
one can talk about being a good soldier instead of a bad soldier.
This is about transformation; this is not about reform. And this
is where the gulf is: between the way I talk and the way I behave.

. . . .

In the microcosm of man there is the resonating higher intelligence that is the model of the higher intelligence of the universe.
One is talking about that level, and that is not unavailable. This is

when something is done *through* one. That's what real doing is. It's not my will, but Thy will. And we can't make it small potatoes. And one doesn't manipulate it. And one doesn't do it by taking oneself by the scruff of the neck and making a demand on oneself. One has to find a way in which one is available to that impulse, to that level of energy. One is not talking about something that is an increase in capacity. One is talking about a new inner reordering that has nothing to do with my ego. This has to do with *I*, with *I am*, not I am this or I am that, but *I am*.

Same Person:
In the meantime, what's going on?

Dr. Welch:
Aren't you working in this way? What do you think you're doing when you're trying to find the inner conditions in your body that make you available to another force? What is that force?

Same Person:
I don't think about it in that way.

Dr. Welch:
Yes, but you're thinking a great deal about this.

Mrs. Welch:
What do you try? Try to be clear about it.

Same Person:
I'll give an example of what I tried, which is a little bit more than what I've been trying all along. It was to see if, in the midst of the day, at specific intervals, I could catch a part of myself. I didn't know how, but I tried sensation. I felt it was a step beyond my attempts at sitting in the morning and in the afternoon, because I felt somehow that the whole day just went by, and I had no touch-stone or signpost as to where I was at the end of the day. It's as if it just took off.

Dr. Welch:
Not "as if."

Same Person:
It *did* take off. And what I discovered was that I forgot. When I remembered, I tried. But I forgot. And it wasn't a cause for regretting, the way I normally regret things. The interesting feature was that I realized something was added to the day, even though I forgot. Because at least I remembered when I forgot. You know, if it was at eight o'clock in the evening, and I remembered at eight-thirty, at least that was something.

Mrs. Welch:
Your memory was short. Is that how you would put it?

But, now, look. Why don't you respond a little differently to the fact that you did remember, even if you were late? You scolded yourself, in a way, for not being absolutely as you had thought you'd undertaken to be. But what does it matter if you're late, if you remember? There's something there that is like punishing yourself for not being orderly—some notion that you have—instead of saying, "All right, I'm remembering it now. What is work?"

Same Person:
I had experiences unconnected with these events, I think, which were extraordinary. But they weren't based on a promise to myself that I would try something four times a day.

Mrs. Welch:
You have a hunger for order, which we all have in a certain way, but the way in which you interpret that order is clock time, instead of being glad whenever you wake up and remember. There's something very important for you there, if you can find your way to it, because you mean this. It isn't just something that you would like to be able to do. It has to do with something very essential for you. That's what I feel, anyway.

Same Person:
The striking thing is, that although I may find myself in many situations where there is a certain kind of attention in operation, it's not the attention that I'm seeking. It's a trained or conditioned attention, which is very important and useful, but it's not attention of *self*.

Mrs. Welch:
But it's already something. Maybe you can make use of it.

Dr. Welch:
It's not conscious attention. We don't have conscious attention, except under very difficult circumstances. We have the attention of the body, the attention of the feelings, the attention of the head, but not all three.

Fourth Questioner:
You spoke of a passion for understanding the meaning and aim of existence. I tried to be aware of how that fell on me, because I've been asking myself what it is that I need. I can't honestly say that that's a real question yet, but tonight I'm trying to stay with it. And I see that there is a fear about knowing what my need is.

I'm talking about two kinds of needs. The first is the inner need to understand. At this moment the best way I can formulate it is: "What is it that I wish to understand before I die?" My other question is: "What is my need in terms of an outer direction, within the Work?" I'm not sure I'm being clear, but...

Dr. Welch:
You know, there's something that's missing here, because I don't think you heard everything in that statement. It is, "In essence, man is a passion..." And here we are searching around in our egos, and our personalities, and our minds, and our associations, and so on. But this is an essential thing, which you may be in touch with only sometimes. It's not the bookkeeper in us. And what is essence?

Same Person:
Well, I think I understand that, a little, when I put it this way:
"How would I serve the Lord?"

Dr. Welch:
That's right. But *who* wants to serve the Lord?

Same Person:
If you were to tell me, "Now, this is how you could serve the Lord,"
that would scare the dickens out of me, but…

Dr. Welch:
It used to be said that *I* want to serve the Lord. The ego has no interest in serving the Lord. But the ego is galloping up the San Juan Hill of
the spirit: "Do-be-do-be-do. Look at me go. And I'm really working."

Serve whom? "I" is not available, except when all this ding-
dong calms itself and it begins to be less demanding, less in
charge. Then something can appear. And then there's no problem,
and one isn't full of arguments and explanations. It's a very clarified situation. It's not the logistical plan of action.

It isn't something that one can manipulate, but there are inner
conditions that one can try for, without trying, in which another
opening exists. But we're not talking about accomplishing something, but rather allowing something to appear that is otherwise
covered over with all kinds of busyness.

And you know that, in the presence of somebody like Mme de
Salzmann, it doesn't seem complicated. It's quite clear. You can't
remember when you get out of the room, but it's clear while you
were there, which tells you something about the nature of it. It's a
real move. Good God, it's magic. It's not something else.

And it's not cheap. And it isn't something that we can utilize.
But it's something that exists in man. And the only difficulty is
that it's there, and I'm not. But it certainly is not a psychological
exercise. It's not wrenching oneself apart. It may be a struggle,
and it may be work, and it may mean suffering. It may mean many
things, but it's not cheap.

Same Person:
Well, I guess that's the level of my question.

Dr. Welch:
Sure it is.

Same Person:
I feel that I now have more of an emotional wish to understand the ideas of the Work, as they relate to a deeper wish, to some meaning from my own life. I don't know where that impulse is, and it certainly isn't a higher impulse. And I also know once I undertake something, even if it is a high impulse, I would see the ego coming from the other direction to meet me. But I feel that that is of the order of things, that I...

Dr. Welch:
Where one stands aside from accomplishment, which is the ego at work.

Same Person:
There is a hunger there, I would say.

Dr. Welch:
Yes, there is. Yes.

Same Person:
But there's something in me that pulls back.

Dr. Welch:
It's true. It's not so easy; it's a pretty dangerous place.

Same Person:
Yes, I think I'm a bit of a perfectionist, and I don't want to see myself undertaking this and not succeeding.

Dr. Welch:
There are all kinds of ways of resisting. "Not so fast." [whispering, as if to oneself]

Same Person:
Yes. But there is still a hunger, which maybe I'm not open to enough.

Mrs. Welch:
I think your gratitude for that hunger is operating in you. It's beginning to demand that you try to work in the direction of an effort to see more clearly. Now, the question always comes to everyone: "What shall I undertake?" How to find what is most useful for you? Sometimes it even has to do with relations with other people, and one has to struggle with the negativities we have, the difficulties, and so on.

I feel very much that you're moving in the right direction, also emotionally.

Same Person:
There's certainly work in Movements that touches something for me.

Mrs. Welch:
One can learn a great deal from the Movements; there's no question about it. I feel you're very much on the right track. You're investigating. You're trying to find, and you will.

Fifth Questioner:
Earlier in the day, when I was sitting, for a few minutes I had a sense of a kind of transparency. I could sense my own body and hear what was going on around me without there being much in the way of thought processes. I had the sense then that the thought processes are somewhat like cotton, always in the way, and in their absence there's this sense of transparency.

I was trying tonight to see if I could stay with that, off and on, while still listening to what was being said. It has always puzzled me how thinking seems to be at odds with a sense of transparency. In a way, I was trying to see whether it's necessary to think. I mean it's clear that I can listen to people and understand English without making any effort. That registers automatically, if I listen. And what became clear, off and on, a little bit, was this drive to have an opinion.

Mrs. Welch:
That's very interesting.

Same Person:
Occasionally, when somebody would say something that had an effect on me emotionally, I'd laugh or have some other reaction. Just for moments, I could see that, without letting it make an opinion, which is what it wanted to do. The push for all of my emotional reactions to produce opinions is almost irresistible— or *is* irresistible.

Dr. Welch:
That's better.

Same Person:
But there's a sense that it's possible for that not to happen. And, in those moments, those emotional reactions become perceptions, in a sense, because they're not short-circuited.

Mrs. Welch:
It always interests me when someone is trying experiments in the way you describe. Sometimes one learns a great deal from that. Sometimes it doesn't give as much, but I think all these interventions can help one's capacity to see more clearly what is going on in oneself and where the difficulties lie. I feel that that is the right direction, trying to be clearer about it, more dispassionate.

Sixth Questioner:
I have a question about level of being. The other night, I had an incident with my daughter, a conversation, if you want to call it that.

Dr. Welch:
A spirited conversation?

Same Person:
The fact of the matter is that she's growing up, and something is coming alive inside of her. I feel that part of the reason that I'm here is to have children and pass something on. And it occurred to me, while this exchange was going on, and while I was trying to be aware of myself, that this is something that is very real for me. And that, somehow, it's what I'm looking for—this immediacy of life. So, even though this was, in fact, not a pleasant exchange, I felt my role as a father. I was trying to impart something real, and I felt that, at the level of my being, I wasn't really able to. Of course, I see in her all the things that she's picked up from me.

Dr. Welch:
Yes. It's a terrible thing, but, you know, children don't hear what you say. It goes in one ear and it goes out the other. All they respond to is how you are. And this is our great deficit. We are not present. We try, but we haven't done our homework. It isn't available to us under the pressure of the event.

Same Person:
In the moment, I know this situation is real. I know it's going on, and yet, I can only act to a certain level. I can only try. And I feel that, yes, I haven't done my homework. I haven't lived a life that is slowly built on experiences so that I am something. My thought is that I'll live however many years, and acquire some experiences, and I'll get smarter. And that I'll be able to really live my life. But it's not happening that way.

Dr. Welch:
Where are all the grownups?

Same Person:
I mean, somehow I have this picture that at the end of my life, I want to be a wise grandfather, you know?

Dr. Welch:
Well, there are a lot of teenagers around producing grandchildren for aspirant grandfathers. You'll get your wish one of these days—before you know it. But you won't be old. [laughter]

Same Person:
Mostly I believe in this other life that I live. That's really where I am most of the time. It lives me, and I'm gone. And then when I'm really in front of something that counts, where, hopefully, I have the opportunity to impart what little I know—or don't know... So, I wonder, how does one acquire being?

Mrs. Welch:
That's the question, all right.

Dr. Welch:
Sure.

Same Person:
And at the same time, I see that I want to cheat. I want to cheat God, you know. I don't know the Bible very well, but I keep this fantasy that I can go out and live my life as crooked as I want it to be.

Dr. Welch:
"God is not mocked. As you sow, you reap."[1] He took care of that in the scriptures. He shortened all that advice. He is not mocked.

1   Galatians 6:7 "God is not mocked: for whatsoever a man soweth, that shall he also reap."

Same Person:
But somehow I think I can cheat.

Dr. Welch:
Yes, I know. The assertion is that He is not mocked. "As you sow, you reap."

Same Person:
But somehow I...

Dr. Welch:
You're convinced that you can get around it, eh?

Same Person:
No, I know, at the same time, that it starts right now. If I want to pay, then I have to start paying. Every day.

Dr. Welch:
Sure. You have to have the right currency, too.

Same Person:
Every day goes by, and I haven't paid. And I figure, well, I'll figure out some way or... You know what I mean?

Dr. Welch:
Yes, I know very well. Yeah. [much laughter]

Same Person:
You know, certain things only go around once, and when you're twelve or thirteen... There's something that's available to her then.

Dr. Welch:
It's true.

Same Person:
And you want them to have it.

Dr. Welch:
And they can't hear.

Same Person:
Yes, it's true. And I was aware of that as well. I could see her eyes and...

Dr. Welch:
They're glazing over. "There he goes again. The old man's jabbering. He's off his rocker."

Mrs. Welch:
Well, you wouldn't be a father without it. I think it's just absolutely inevitable.

Dr. Welch:
But it verifies so clearly that this is not words. We've got a lot of words.

Mrs. Welch:
[after a pause] What do you want to do? To inspire them or to control them? There's a big question there.

Dr. Welch:
You want to give them something that can't be given. You want them to, at least, understand what you understand. And this isn't transferable. There's no way to give them experiential, substantive knowledge—something that we know in our bones, because we have embodied it, literally embodied it. There's a great difference between talk and being.

Same Person:
And also, it's a reflection on my own life.

Dr. Welch:
Well, it's a reflection on the level of our being. I don't think of myself as an example of a level of being. I think of myself as the

center of the universe, as the unique experience, as the one true observer—Mr. Right.

Same Person:
Everyone in this room thinks of you that way. [laughter]

Dr. Welch:
I would like to be serious about this. Because everybody in this room feels this way about themselves. I'm not talking about what they say about themselves. But how they act—how *we* act—in relation to life. The central romance, the central experience, is *mine*. It may not be all that great all the time, but, nonetheless, all of it is *terribly* important. And I am confronted by the opposite poles of being the center of the universe and the idea that I'm practically non-existent, practically zero—this business of nothingness that I don't really accept. I can really almost visualize this—that even here in New York, I'm only one seven-millionth part.

The fact is that I am the center of everything. Everything that I know about the world, about myself, goes on in me. It doesn't go on out there on a screen. Now, this is inescapable, and one's opinion of oneself is unimportant. Whatever the opinion is, one's life is *the central reality*. And everything, whether I see it or not, takes place inside me.

Same Person:
I'm trying to understand what you're saying. My experience is that there are a few moments of my life that are really my life, and that the rest of it is squandered or missed or slept through or dreamed or...

Dr. Welch:
Yes, but it's not somewhere else, it's in you. It's all in you; everything is contained in you. It isn't outside you. That's your data about the whole enterprise. You can't live anybody else's life. You can't really know what goes on inside of anybody else, and everything that's out there is hearsay. In here is your life.

This is the inner knowledge, of whatever character. And what you may read in a book, that's not in you. You may learn to embody some idea that you read in a book and become the *manifestation* of this. But you're talking about what's going on in you, and it doesn't go on in me. Mine goes on in me.

MARCH 22, 1991

Essence and personality. The wonder of the human organism.

First Questioner:

I have a question about this endeavor that we are engaged in. There are certain kinds of experiences in the Work that we talk about as being given, as coming from outside of ourselves.

The phrase "the face of God" kept coming to me all week long, as a question. And it evoked something in me that made me question very deeply what comes from me and what is already there. It's as if something is in me, but independent of me.

Dr. Welch:

You know, I think I hear something here that wishes to make sure that one doesn't get deluded by a proprietary sense of initiation, a proprietary sense of possession. One is a cornucopia of gifts; everything is a gift. There is a great variety of essential realities in man. My God, you can—without expanding too broadly, perhaps—state that one's capacity for intelligence is a gift. How would you or I begin to invent or know something about how to approach speech, thought, weighing, comparing, listening? All these things are gifts. No amount of training could give me the skill you have with a paintbrush. And I'm not being flattering about this. You didn't learn all that, at the same time that you did. But you had a capacity for it. Fred Astaire didn't really learn to dance; he couldn't not dance. If he'd been born in Russia, he'd have been Nureyev, but he happened to have been born in Omaha, Nebraska.

Same Person:
But it seems that these were the things that we were talking about last Friday, that our personalities...

Dr. Welch:
Well, I'm talking about essence now.

Mrs. Welch:
There's a difference.

Dr. Welch:
These are essential, although you may not think of them as being "that thing we call essence." [affecting a deep, serious voice] Everything that is acquired is personality, but the way and the capacity to acquire are essential. Do you understand the distinction? It's what you're born with. It's your genetic mix. And this is a scrambled egg, if you will. If you have a notion of essence and personality, you have a place from which, not to know all about it, but to think about it. No amount of fabrication and artful conditioning can produce a brain surgeon out of just anybody. There are those people who have the capacity for this kind of highly sensitive stuff. And you know very well when they don't have this quality. It's a dreadful thing to watch. You don't want a brain surgeon with a tremor.

I think this idea of essence and personality is a very useful frame from which to have some notion about our gifts. You know, the greatest example that I can summon up at the moment is Mozart. Nobody taught Mozart to run up a concerto when he was eight years old. This is essential.

Same Person:
When I thought about it, I didn't think about it in terms of essence and personality, but rather that something is attracted towards a right order. It's as if some part of me knows what it is to be alive. It's as if there's something that's known. I don't quite know how to describe it, really. And maybe it is simply, as you

say—when one paints, for instance, in my case—that that is as it should be.

Dr. Welch:
It's harmonious.

Same Person:
It's harmonious.

Dr. Welch:
That doesn't include the time when the gears shift, and you are suddenly connected with something else, so that it becomes this plus something that plays on you. I think the concept of the muse is helpful. You make a connection with a higher capacity in yourself. It is what all real jazz musicians are doing when they're improvising. They're all working and playing and playing, trying to get to that same point. It's what every artist has been touched by. But these are levels of inner connections, because man begins by being incomplete. That doesn't mean that he doesn't experience a level of intelligence in himself, sometimes—a level of feeling-perception, sometimes. And this is a moment of inner movement upward.

We say upward because that's where everything good is supposed to be—near the top. Why we just assume that it's up there and not inside a circle, coming out like a radius, I don't know. But these are the terms we have for it.

Same Person:
I think my real question is why, when you see the face of God, you recognize it. It's as if you knew it all along. It can be playing jazz, or painting, or sitting here right now, or in any moment. But I didn't acquire that. It's as if one recognizes it; it's as if one knows.

Dr. Welch:
Well, yes. Everything one knows anything about, anything that one experiences, must, per force, take place inside, because this is the only place where it can be experienced. But one is not alone.

One is not self-conceived or self-created, and one doesn't know what the connections are in oneself that have a resonance on another level of intelligence, another level of knowing, of awareness, of indeed—what you spoke of earlier—being alive. These are mysteries of the universe. But, of course, we take ourselves for granted, and yet we're mobile miracles, for God's sake, of the most incredible foresight and fabrication. It's astounding that everybody in this room is a miracle. We don't think so because we take it all for granted, but the truth is that we're beautifully complicated, elegantly refined, and extraordinarily capable of the most astonishing nuances of inner machinery.

It's all like a lot of living cobwebs in there. There's no excess, there's no overkill. Well, there are more ova in the ovaries than the world will ever need, more sperm than the world will ever need. And this is fascinating, in a way, that there is this kind of abundance of life.

But one little hole in the right blood vessel, or one little plug in the wrong blood vessel, and the whole damn thing turns into a hulk. But while it's got its pipes in order, and hasn't run its course, it's miraculous. And you can't reduce it to a nosebag inside that's filled, and that's all there is to it. The truth is that we don't start out... What's more useless than a newborn baby?

Mrs. Welch:
What's more adorable?

Dr. Welch:
Well, that's another question. But, you know, they're no damn good for anything. They're just tubes, open at both ends. Everything there in order? [simulates slapping a newborn] And that's it. But give them a chance to be pumped up, as time goes on, and let them grow... They *grow*! Can you believe that? We take it for granted that they'll grow. And when they get to a certain point, they will stop growing. And they won't go on up through the ceiling. It's amazing. They know just how fast and how far to go. The legs get so long, just long enough to reach the ground. Fin-

gers don't go bleeeuuuuuugh. It's amazing, you know. Absolutely astounding.

Mrs. Welch:
You have to have a great respect for nature, yes?

Dr. Welch:
Oh, my God! Can you imagine being programmed that far in advance? To be as old as we are and yet not fallen apart? It's astounding. I think anybody who ever looks at a healing wound... How does it know when to stop healing?

I don't know what one does with this sense of being staggered by the reality of it all. But at least it doesn't fail to awaken a little sense of the forethought of somebody. I feel a little bit like Hassein.

*Negativity. "Anything that helps." Breathing. Punishing oneself.
When work makes sense.*

First Questioner:
It seems to me that I am noticing the inherent negativity of my ordinary state. There is no good reason for it, and it has no particular form.

Dr. Welch:
What kind of negativity is it?

Same Person:
Little things. For example, being angry at this person about something, and an impatient attitude about that one, and always justifying it, and...

Dr. Welch:
What's beneath it?

Same Person:
I'm not sure I know what's beneath it, but I can say that after proper conditions or a real effort, that it disappears for a while. Well, I think I know what is beneath it, but it's too easy in a sense to say, because I don't see it very well, but I think fear is beneath it.

Dr. Welch:
Yes. It occurred to me—and I think I've verified it many times—that the only basis on which one has a kind of prevailing negative attitude toward everything is when there is an underlying anxi-

ety, or depression, or fear, or sense of dislocation, or maybe some considering that is deeply related to some upcoming endpoint. Because one lives mostly with immediate endpoints: with appointments, with things that have to be done, or things that are going to threaten, and so on. And from an opposite point of view, there are inner conditions in which you can't get angry at anyone. There is no possibility, in this case, of an emotional reaction. These negativities are not the result of those outside us that we can't stand, but rather are really derived from an emotional tone in us that colors everything.

Same Person:
I would say that anxiety is a good one...

Dr. Welch:
Anxiety is a good one, yes, because nobody's free of that in one way or another, in whatever form, and this *is* a form of fear. And it's a property of the ego, not of the essence, if you like.

Second Questioner:
Anxiety is a property of the ego?

Dr. Welch:
As distinct from "I." As distinct from another state. It may be better to say egoism. It's related to one's image of oneself.

First Questioner:
It certainly involves the future.

Dr. Welch:
Yes. The threat.

Same Person:
The ego wants to think about the future all the time, and what's upcoming, and then thinks about it more than necessary.

Third Questioner:
How much of that has to do with habit, with imitation that begins early on in life?

Dr. Welch:
I think we learn how to be this way from our models. You hear little kids in the street talking like their angry mothers, you know? You hear this all the time. You can practically see the shrew that they imitated, with characteristically semi-vulgar ways of saying whatever it is about how you are, or what you're doing, or what you ought not to do. We haven't got any better models than that.

Same Person:
I'm so glad this was raised, because, of course, it's something that I deal with in my life, as most everybody does, but I have a very strong habit of it.

The one I mostly learned it from was my mother, who was a very unhappy woman, and though she could not get angry and burst out, she was critical of everyone, and of many things. Not that she couldn't be positive and joyous, but she spent, I think, a great part of her life in that negative state.

The only time I really got very angry at her was when I was an adult and I wanted to shock her. And she got, I guess you would say, catatonic. She froze, and I promised myself I would never fight with her again. And I have, in some ways, avoided confrontation in my life (except when I feel safe, like with my poor children).

But it's such a wonderful thing that this was brought, because it's very important to get to see that about myself, or how we develop in that way, because it goes on from generation to generation.

Dr. Welch:
But it's possible for you to find a space in yourself toward your mother that is sympathetic. You didn't know when you were a little girl that she too was a victim. She too was vulnerable and was an example of the human muddle, you know? I remember very

vividly when it suddenly dawned on me that my mother and father were not monuments. They were not statues, they were not institutions, they were not fixed icons, but were suffering human beings, like everybody else.

Fourth Questioner:
How old were you?

Dr. Welch:
Oh God, I don't know, but I certainly wasn't young, probably past middle age. But the whole idea of being able to forgive your parents struck me then. It seemed to me it was an aspect of growing up. One comes to it; it doesn't have to be forced or contrived. One suddenly sees—if one sees enough of oneself—that, of course, they were in a bind, in a trap. And when they were warm and active and positive, they felt safe, and when they were otherwise, they were, in one way or another, stalked by some dark fear. And you cannot not bleed for them. You know?

. . . .

We've been instructed, in a way, to be suspicious of this negativity, whereas in an ordinary way, there's a popular notion that negativity is evidence of character. "He's strict, he's critical, because, by God, he has standards!" You know? But I think that with the worldview of Gurdjieff, which has been pretty well "osmosed" into us, in one way or another, we don't welcome or misinterpret this, and we recognize that one is suffering—in a modest way, but nonetheless, one is in a state of something that is certainly not open or available, and is constricted, and is destructive, in its way.

First Questioner:
I recognize it in retrospect, anyway. At the time, I almost welcome it.

Dr. Welch:
Yes. At the time one is taken by it. It isn't so easy to break that. But regardless of how much one is a slave or victim of the horse, in retrospect—or, indeed, in one's general attitude—one doesn't say, or think, that it's evidence of a rigorous attitude, and that it speaks of character. We have the feeling that it speaks of a kind of vulnerable weakness. And we have been told, and rather suspect, that we are also capable of exulting in this—that business of falling in love with one's negativity. It's not easy to be sure that one knows what that really means, but it is astonishing how one can become attached to it.

Mrs. Welch:
That's a way of dealing with fear, isn't it? If I'm not afraid of anybody, I can be just as disagreeable as I want to be. I'm that much stronger.

Dr. Welch:
Yes. It's a strange, strange business, if true. And it seems to have certain verifiable aspects, in any event. But it certainly is not a big thing. It's a powerful thing, but it's not on a heroic scale; it's on a picky scale, a small scale.

Fifth Questioner:
I'd like to ask about something that is on a different subject, I think. And it's about the head, as opposed to what I'm calling the subconscious, although I don't really know what that is. I have three examples of this. In Movements, rhythms are very difficult for me. I'm not saying I'm different from anybody else, but it's very difficult to do a different hand rhythm from a foot rhythm. At the beginning of this year, I decided that my effort there would be not to give in to my frustration, but to just force myself to try as best I could. And I find that sometimes I can do this, but as soon as I start to think about it, or analyze it, it's gone and I can't do it anymore. So this is...

Mrs. Welch:
Moving center?

Same Person:
Yes. That the head has no place here is what I feel about that. The head interferes.

I see now that the other two experiences are different, but... I was on the phone at the office and talking to somebody, and it occurred to me that I should ask where they were. And then my head said, "Well, I don't need to know," and I hung up. Then somebody called and asked, "Do you know where so-and-so is?" And I said, "Well, I just spoke with her, but I'm sorry, I don't." Perhaps it was some kind of common sense or something else—it wasn't the head anyway. And I thought afterward that I should have trusted this, wherever that came from.

And this week, because of our meeting last week and various other feelings, I have tried to sit every morning and for a longer time, which I haven't done on a regular basis recently. And I have felt that it has made a difference to my day. This morning it was very difficult to relax, but I just kept trying, and I felt that what I needed to do was simply to say "hallelujah." And so I said, "hallelujah." I sang, "hallelujah." And doing this relaxed part of me that wasn't relaxed before.

And then I started thinking about it: "How does that relate to my life? How could I have a praise of God in my life, and how does that relate to what I think of as the Work?" This sudden idea of "hallelujah" is what I need, instead of trying once more in the same way, you know?

Dr. Welch:
Tighten up and relax.

Same Person:
Yes.

Mrs. Welch:
Well, there's also the idea of making use of anything that helps.

Dr. Welch:
Yes, I was just thinking, "All's fair in love and war."

Mrs. Welch:
If you have certain associations that you have from childhood, or from wherever they originated, why not utilize them? And in addition, the sound of that itself carries a certain impulse. There is something in the pronunciation that can wake you up for a moment.

Dr. Welch:
Changes the scale.

Mrs. Welch:
I think it does, yes.

Same Person:
It was just there. It wasn't...

Dr. Welch:
Yes, it wasn't an idea.

Same Person:
No.

Dr. Welch:
There's a reason for liturgical music, and I think one discovers that there's a liturgical connotation in the Movements music. It doesn't have a liturgy, but it associates. The music is a call. It summons one, in a way. And it awakens a resonance in one that has to do with aspiration.

It just occurred to me, as I was thinking of this, that there's a long recognition in human affairs that this melodic upward movement has an elevating quality that changes the tightly personal state. It summons one's aspiration and awakens the connection that one has to a reality larger than the fact that one is uptight.

Mrs. Welch:

You know, it's interesting, what you're saying, because I've been thinking lately about the effect of rhythm. How different our rhythms are, for instance, when we're crossing the street in a hurry than when we're doing something in Movements. If we really understood it better, if we studied it, we could begin to see what rhythms are necessary to get us into a certain frame of mind.

Dr. Welch:

Yes. Yes, I'm sure of that.

Mrs. Welch:

There's something so definite about it that we ought to know. Dancers know it to some degree.

Dr. Welch:

And then there's the question of where the places are where one hears this note, this resonance, this rhythm, this tone. It isn't just in your ear, you know. I think these things are heard in the solar plexus.

Sixth Questioner:

I was in Movements yesterday and there was a Movement where we were saying "Lord, have mercy" out loud, which later was only to be said inside. It was said with the sensation in different limbs, and then "I am." And it came with the music. And I had this feeling that I had never dared to really try to engage myself in something like that. But the words have meaning, and it was possible then. And there was just this flash of memory of so many different things that have been given. In a way, I think my characteristic attitude is "I'm learning this. Later I'll understand it, and then I'll really try. Some other time it will be appropriate." And the only time is now.

. . . .

Seventh Questioner [a physician]:
I've noticed in sitting that my breathing seems to be a very sensitive instrument for seeing where I am. If I'm relaxing, centered, and a little bit present, then it slows down. Sometimes, to levels where I wonder...

Dr. Welch:
If you're really ventilating properly?

Same Person:
Yes, whether I'm suppressing it somehow. Though I don't feel I am. But then a thought comes—an association—and I'll be off, you know, arguing with somebody. And when I come back to a more gathered state, the breathing has changed. It can be fifteen seconds, and it's all different.

Dr. Welch:
It's difficult, it seems to me, not to believe that one breathes intentionally. My breathing goes on quite without my intentional intervention. It's not to say that I can't, but I don't. And what is interesting, it seems to me, is that the mechanical ventilation, with the upward thrust of the thorax and the inhalation by virtue of air pressure—not by virtue of my inhaling—just takes place.

Mrs. Welch:
The intelligence of the body, that I'm hardly aware of most of the time...so extraordinary, isn't it, that it varies its rhythm as necessary and even senses when more air is required?

Dr. Welch:
When you see that the breathing goes on with its own life, in sleep... It always fascinates me, when you see somebody asleep and hear their breathing, that it's taking care of itself. It's just not a volitional business of any kind.

And I've only delivered, I don't know, a dozen or so kids, but that business of their first real inhalation is a great thing. [imitates it]

Fifth Questioner:
I've had this same experience with the breathing. Isn't it an example of how what you're thinking and feeling really does affect your body, and that you don't usually know it? The stronger experience for me is getting caught up in something and then remembering, and realizing I'm all tense, when I wasn't before. And presumably the tension came because I'd just had that imaginary argument with somebody. What struck me this week is that unless you are actually trying to do something, you don't notice any of this; it all just goes on. You only see it when you're sitting, or when you're trying to do something.

Mrs. Welch:
When you're watching, really—to some degree.

Same Person:
Yes.

Dr. Welch:
At such a moment, one has an experience of self-observation. Or, if not that, at least one can say it is self-awareness. One is not as lost in it. It's more nearly a sidelong glance. One doesn't interfere with it, or have notions of how it ought to be, but one is aware of it—more nearly as an observer.

Third Questioner:
I've been trying to understand more about what Mme de Salzmann said in some readings—and I think Mr. Gurdjieff may have said it also—that if one doesn't really try to make an effort at presence, one should punish oneself. The fact is that I remain totally mechanical, and when I see that, something takes place. Even if it's only for an instant, something is more there. But I'm not really able to punish myself in the sense that somebody said: not have any supper or something like that. I really am not.

Mrs. Welch:
Well, it's only when you undertake something specifically. If I decide I'm going to pay attention to some manifestation, and then I forget, then it is necessary to help me to remember, when I try again.

Dr. Welch:
It's a very tricky business, I think, this question of punishing yourself. Mme de Salzmann often qualifies this by saying that it's not torturing yourself. It's not such nonsense. But a deprivation of something that you're accustomed to assuage your body with, something you like, something that you'll miss, can be the mildest sort of remonstrance. But it's largely because you can't forget it. It usually means interrupting some habitual way of entertaining oneself, or of responding to some appetitive aspect of oneself. But it's very tricky, because there are all kinds of stupid self-disciplines that one can impose on oneself for all the wrong reasons. And this quickly can become a peacock feather instead of a reminding factor.

. . . .

Eighth Questioner:
I tried several times this week to be aware of myself, of my sensations, mostly while walking or driving, for a certain distance. I hadn't decided on any particular time. It's just that it occurs to me a few times a day, and then I'll decide to try it. I was very struck, because sometimes—and the minority of the time—I'll walk for whatever distance it is, and see my thoughts pulling me away, and fend them off, and come back, and stay with myself pretty much for that short distance. But frequently that's not possible; the thoughts will take me. What strikes me is that the ingredient that makes it possible, or not, is something about which I have really no comprehension. It seems to occur, or not occur, in very much the same circumstances. Sometimes there's something that catches my interest, some little spark that makes it possible. And

frequently that spark just isn't there, even though I still try to come back.

Dr. Welch:
When that spark is there, it makes sense, and you're interested, and it isn't about doing your push-ups.

Mrs. Welch:
That makes all the difference, doesn't it?

Dr. Welch:
I think it's the heart of the matter.

Same Person:
I know you've said things like this, and I tend to react, and say, "I'll just do it." It doesn't have to be a very big spark.

Dr. Welch:
It's two centers instead of one. That's what it is. And it's got a third one working for it. It's more nearly whole. And this is another state. And it isn't because one is sometimes ornery and at other times more agreeable. You know, it's that thing we keep spinning: "In order to get there, you have to be there." It's true. We have to be at a certain level in ourselves in order for this to make any sense at all. Otherwise, it's a completely intellectual instruction. Something in your head reminds you that you are really subject to an inner discipline, and you'd better demonstrate it—which is just so much junk.

Same Person:
I know when it happens, or doesn't happen, but what struck me particularly was that I really have no sense, when the thought occurs to me, and I say, for example, "Well, I'll try now for this block," of whether or not it's going to set off that spark. Sometimes it does, and sometimes it doesn't.

Mrs. Welch:

Isn't that interesting, when you know somewhere, that you're more interested in yourself than anyone else in the world? Each of us has that. Here I am on the planet Earth, for a short time. Who am I? What takes place? We all have that. Now why don't I make use of that interest? Am I always so busy trying to make an impression on other people? Do you think that's partly it? And yet I think, as we get older, we get less interested in that.

Dr. Welch:

Mmmm mmmm [wondering whether what Mrs. Welch last said is true]

Same Person:

It's amazing how much power it has, despite the fact that I'm not interested in it.

First Questioner:

I guess scale comes into it a lot, because, in my ordinary way, it's me, trying to get through life, and that really has no sense to it.

Dr. Welch:

That's right.

Same Person:

The other scale is my being part of this mystery, doing whatever I do, and it doesn't really matter what.

Dr. Welch:

How do you consider internally never, externally always?

Same Person:

You have to remember the scale...

Dr. Welch:

You have to be somewhere beyond the preoccupation with these charming masquerades.

First Questioner:
During the Movements class that I help with, when the other instructor was teaching, I was finding it difficult to really watch people, to see what their difficulty was, what would be needed, what we could bring, and so on. I have a tendency to get tense in that situation, wanting the class to do it differently, wanting it to be different than what it is. And I'm not really able to look at the people and wonder what their experience might be.

Then there was this little moment that occurred. I began to try to feel in myself what the exercise that had been proposed would require, what the effort was that the class was being asked to make. As soon as that connection was made, I was able to watch with no difficulty at all. It struck me that it's not just the other person and myself. There isn't an engagement, in a certain way, until it's the pursuit that is important, when the Movement itself becomes important. When I became interested in the Movement, in the exercise, then I could watch and see, without tension and without embarrassment.

Dr. Welch:
And what do you think was the difference?

Same Person:
That I was concerned about the exercise and not considering. It seemed, in retrospect, that it was because I became interested inside myself in what was being asked of the class.

Dr. Welch:

But what you've said is that something about the Movement, something about your engagement with the Movement, changed the place from which you were looking at it. I think this is right at the heart of the whole enterprise. Something changed in your attitude toward that Movement, and it would not be wrong to say that it was a change in level. And that's what we're talking about. Something about the Movement's significance, something about its message, something about its connection, helped lift your state from one of preoccupation, and tension, and nervousness, and considering—all the junk that characterizes us. Then you found yourself able to *be there* in another way. You didn't initiate it; it took place. And one can't manipulate it anyway. But something contrived to make it possible for you to be in touch with that Movement in a very different way from that of a drill sergeant. It made you nervous to be a drill sergeant; you knew that was stupid.

Same Person:

I wasn't actually teaching.

Dr. Welch:

No, I know, but you were watching from the point of view of how well they were doing it.

Same Person:

Yes, that's exactly it.

Dr. Welch:

And this made you uncomfortable. One doesn't have to inflate these things, but you were in another place in yourself when you began to see the Movement. And perhaps it is not fantasy to say that maybe this was the action of the Movement on you.

Same Person:

Later, when it was my turn to teach, this continued, and I did things that I hadn't planned to, and they worked. It must have come from a perception of what was needed. The Foundation wasn't cooled at all earlier this week, and the heat changed my plans. So, it was partly as a result of that, but, nevertheless, I've very rarely felt free enough to change what I decided to do ahead of time, based on being able to trust what the moment tells me.

Mrs. Welch:
Were you very aware of the difference? Did you feel that it took place in you organically?

Same Person:
I was struck at the time.

Mrs. Welch:
It's something that I don't think we talk about very much, but we must experience it: the *power* of a true observation, when you really *see* what is taking place, which I think is the underlying reason for undertaking the art of self-observation.

Dr. Welch:
And the importance of that inner shift. One tends not to appreciate the change in the inner order that made your observation quite different. It's silly to fantasize about that, but, nonetheless, you had a little whiff of *being* differently in yourself. It was another ordering of something that included a larger part of yourself, without that preoccupation.

Same Person:
And without fear. I remember you commented on that as a characteristic.

Dr. Welch:
Yes. Fear is such a devil.

Mrs. Welch:

Well, the thing that shot through my head was one thing that Mme de Salzmann said: "The Work works." Here she had an experience that the Work works. And it sometimes takes you by surprise. Who is it in oneself that made the decision to work? It isn't the usual head thing that allows us to work.

Dr. Welch:

The fact that it takes place should, could, might—if it were sufficiently appreciated—be welcomed. And it might be the place from which this sort of undertaking could be the aspiration, the occasion, for remembering. Because one wishes to speak from *that*, rather than from what Gurdjieff always called wiseacreing: being deftly rational, and wondering why the fruit has no juice.

One is really in the dark, in a way, about this. The most difficult question is "When you work, what do you do?" Mme de Salzmann was an expert at that. "Speak about your work," she used to say.

Second Questioner:

I would like to bring an observation. I was standing out in front of the house, and the weather was changing. It was getting cooler, and the wind was coming in and really blowing. It must have been the weather, but I looked, and it's as if I saw the buildings in a new light. I knew they were the same old buildings, but I never saw them that way. It's as if they were very special. I don't know how to explain it. It was just magical, and I was struck by that. And I tried to stay with that. It didn't last long, but it lasted long enough to raise the question of what was missing...

Dr. Welch:

...before. It's so clear, isn't it?

Same Person:

I had the attitude of "stinky, smelly New York," and I wished the wind would blow harder so I could get rid of that smell. And then, all of a sudden, it was nothing like the stinky, smelly New York. It was alive. The cars were not just chunks of metal; they had a place. The people walking the streets were no longer just intruders on my terrain. All of this changed as if someone had turned the light on, and the light had been off prior to that.

Fear was mentioned earlier. It was interesting, in that I didn't know that I was in a state of considering until I was not in a state of considering—about the people, the meeting that was coming up, and all of that. It was as if I was in this involvement, and then I was not involved. It didn't matter how I sat or stood, or how I looked, because it was a beautiful evening.

Dr. Welch:
It's a marvelous thing, that moment of the contrast between one's preoccupied scanning of where one is—knowing all about whatever it is, and not having any impression of it at all—and then that curious reshuffle and one sees, as if for the first time. Then one has an impression of the contrast between levels in oneself.

Mrs. Welch:
And freedom from the usual associations.

Dr. Welch:
Yes, and being free from being totally occupied—having some space in which one receives something, instead of everything being crowded out by one's daydream about things and one's usual preoccupations. To be free of fear for a moment...

Same Person:
There's a certain head knowledge about the lack.

Dr. Welch:
This is not that, though.

Same Person:
It may sometimes precede it. You feel a failure in the face of it,

because you say, "Why is it that it's still this way, this dull way? I'm trying."

Dr. Welch:
And it's all in the head.

Same Person:
Yes, exactly. But this is just a sudden magical transition.

Mrs. Welch:
Why is it that, knowing that we can be free of all the garbage, we return to it all the time? Is it nature that demands it? Do you think it's a form of self-punishment?

Dr. Welch:
No, I don't think it's so much self-punishment as it is resignation. It's a place to hide. It's giving up.

Same Person:
I think resignation is on the mark, because that's what I've been feeling about trying and giving up.

Dr. Welch:
There is no nourishment from the head alone. It relates to what we were saying a little earlier about the logical dissertations on the human state.

Same Person:
The deft rationality.

Dr. Welch:
And at the same time, the trap is that one can begin to imagine that one can leave one's head. And that's nonsense too, because it's the head plus. You need the head. There is this notion that all of the mind is in the way. The ordinary, preoccupied mind is in the way, just as the ordinary emotions are in the way.

Same Person:
I guess this is probably a head question.

Dr. Welch:
Sure, but, you know, what the hell? What else have we got? Where would you be without your head?

Same Person:
I'd be headless.

Dr. Welch:
Yes, you'd be a headless horseman.

Same Person:
It's just that, unless I totally misunderstand it, there is, if you will, the Work idea that our higher centers are perfectly okay. It's our lower centers that are not up to speed. And hence we have this inability to connect. So, I live in my lower centers, whether I'm cognizant of it or not. And I have some sort of precarious balance. Somehow I manage to go to work, and so on.

Dr. Welch:
Well, you were wound up. You can't help it.

Same Person:
There is dissatisfaction in this balance, not permanently and not very...

Dr. Welch:
And not enough dissatisfaction.

Same Person:
Not enough. But there are times when I actually feel the futility of repeating this all the time. And then, all of a sudden, the switch goes on. It's as if, "Oh, yes. This is why." I don't know if the ordinary centers will ever come up to speed. I don't know that I know

what the hell I'm talking about, or doing, or trying. I mean, I used to think, twenty years ago, that somehow I'd get these ordinary centers up to speed.

Dr. Welch:
Well, we have great difficulty with the idea that, somehow or other, I'm going to manipulate this, because it's not very comforting to our self-esteem to entertain the idea that there are other influences—the play of forces, if you like. I don't really believe that. I don't really see myself as dependent on external sources. I think of myself as being active.

Mrs. Welch:
I make the choices.

Dr. Welch:
Yes. And I don't think one gives that up, or should, on someone's say-so. But real doing is "Thy will," and what I call doing is my will. And this is in the realm of desire, of dislike, of like, and so on. Real doing is on another level and requires a higher force, which becomes something active instead of reactive. And I don't think it's easy to settle those notions in one's head. But one sees that this can take place. Transformation is not something that one does, but something that one becomes available to. It's quite another sense of oneself.

Mrs. Welch:
What is it that takes over, then? Is it a moment of relative wisdom? Because it has to do with the degree of self-seeing. It's only when one sees that, and feels that clearly, that something is possible other than just self-criticism.

Dr. Welch:
I like that distinction of "I am" rather than "I am this" and "I am that."

Mrs. Welch:
That's right.

Dr. Welch:
Rather, "I am." Period. Which is a quality of being, rather than a description of my elegant character.

It's very difficult not to be enclosed in one's private world, but it's also foolish to imagine that one isn't.

Mrs. Welch:
After all, it's always one's own response, isn't it? And we're speaking about not being at the mercy of a narrow, limited reaction, but being able to see more and, therefore, experience more.

Dr. Welch:
Yes, it's an interesting thing that the contemporary, positivist, materialist view is that the mind, and whatever we mean by spirit, is a quantitative elaboration of material, of matter, from below upwards. That it is really a refinement of amoebas. The amoeba "tore itself apart and invented sex."

Mrs. Welch:
"Amoebas at the start," did you say?

Dr. Welch:
"Amoebas at the start were not complex; they tore themselves apart and started Sex."

Mrs. Welch:
"And Sex has ruled the lives of clods and kings." Don't forget that.[1]

Dr. Welch:
That really is the heart of the industrial revolution, of Darwin, of

1 This refers to a poem entitled *Sex*, by Arthur Guiterman, that the Welches liked very much. See, for example: https://www.poemhunter.com/poem/sex-38/

Renaissance man, of the physicist: that life started with a lot of random lightning and a lot of potential soup. The interesting thing is that this came first, and that an infinite differentiation of this produced something higher, something of another quality. And the other view is that spirit is there, not here. That man is a microcosm.

Mrs. Welch:
You know, this is something that we don't understand. As you were saying, I could see the Holy Affirming, the Holy Denying, the Holy Reconciling. But we get caught in one of these traps. We don't see the relations, the movement of the forces, on which our entire lives depend.

Dr. Welch:
Yes, it's as if there were no infusion of spirit from whatever source.

Mrs. Welch:
The Holy Affirming, to give it a name.

Dr. Welch:
Well, yes, the Absolute, His Endlessness—all that. But we have been persuaded that spirit is a quantitative change in matter, not a qualitative infusion from another place.

Mrs. Welch:
It's quite another substance.

Same Person:
The view that permeates our society is that the universe somehow is dead or dying.

Dr. Welch:
Yes, matter is dead and energy is random, without sense.

Mrs. Welch:
There's no relation.

Dr. Welch:

The whole thing is a frame of reference that we don't even take into account, because it sounds very strange to talk about a play of forces and a force of another quality, of another character, of another vibration rate, which carries with it this thing that isn't easily measured.

Mrs. Welch:

I was in situations where I met, and had access to, some scientists with brilliant minds. And, although they approached it in terms of thought, for many the question itself became much more important to them, and they began to have the recognition that there was a force that they didn't even know how to approach, let alone understand.

But how does one search for the vibrancy of truth from one's own point of view, one's necessity. It isn't a question of being clever about it—using a lot of equations. I think, more and more, that it has to contain thought and feeling and some variety of direct movement: inner movement that must have an outer manifestation.

There was a question about attention and the difficulty of maintaining it.

Dr. Welch:
Who is in charge of this attention? It can be taken by a feeling. It can be taken by an idea. It can be taken by an association. It can be taken by bodily distress. It certainly is taken by a toothache, a sprained ankle or a broken bone. It's taken by almost anything, from a shop window to a puff of wind.

And there is no use our pretending that our difficulty is not connected with a flawed capacity to attend and to stay. One's experience with attention is that it doesn't last.

But when there is something that we *can't* drop, because it's so threatening, or so engaging, then it can fix us. We are simply glued to a thought we can't drop, an idea we can't let go, somebody who fascinates us, a threat. Name it. It doesn't make any difference. If my interest is caught, I can't *not* attend. Attention is the most important element of my economy, and I am not in touch with it.

Attention has a life of its own. And having some kind of relation to it, or bringing it near to something that I *intend* is not easily comprehended. It is as though it has as independent a life as the liver has, or the kidneys have.

What is the function of attention? It is said that we need, in order to survive, a certain number of impressions each second. Such impressions are received by way of attention. If my attention is not that drawn to an impression, I am apt to miss it. My attention has a way of fulfilling the requirement. It will go to a loud noise. It will go to a whisper. It will go to heat. It will go to pain, to light, to movement. The things that our five senses receive constitute the impressions that we live on.

Now, it is not unreasonable to say that the attention certainly has a big role to play in nature's organism, which is endowed with the capacity to eat ordinary food, to breathe in air, and to receive impressions. These three things make a difference as to whether or not the organism continues to function.

One can demonstrate that impressions are very important. Experiments have been done where one limits the impressions by putting somebody into a bath that is at body temperature so that there isn't any contrast. In these conditions, people get rather psychotic after a while. Clearly, the reception of impressions includes some purpose of nature that has programmed this capacity to be extremely whimsical, and not, by any means, to be readily the slave of my presumed intention.

And all too often, our experiences have a partial nature because our attention is elsewhere. It's not so completely elsewhere that some of it isn't shared by what is taking place, but it isn't a whole perception that stays with the event.

Second Questioner:
It seems to me that I have two types of attention. One is as you have described it. But, at times, I fall into a relationship with some sense of presence, and, in that, there is the taste of a different type of attention that operates at a different speed.

Dr. Welch:
I think that's quite true. What is it? Can one speak of the attention of a level of being that is, let's say, self-conscious, self-aware? The attention of the higher mind is something quite different from our everyday attention. It has another intensity, another capacity. One is really talking about another level of being. This level of being requires a good deal of quiet and an unnatural composure—a quieting of the forces that keep us in motion. And a lot of motion

continues in any event. Breathing continues. The lungs expand and collapse. The heart contracts and relaxes. To hold yourself upright requires a lot of muscular tension. There's a great deal of activity going on, most of which doesn't attract my attention. When I undertake to put my attention on places where I suspect this kind of thing is taking place, I have another sense of myself. But I find it very difficult, because the attention wavers and is taken away.

And what we're really experiencing is the absence of a relationship among the three centers: the head and the body and the feeling. If the feeling is, by chance, quieter, the body less agitated, and the mind less pursued by something that is eating me up, then I have the experience of a quieter ordinary mind, a more relaxed ordinary body, and a connection between the head and the body that began by applying just my ordinary attention. It changes my relation to myself.

If it becomes intense enough, I feel something of quite another order than the feeling of my ordinary emotional life. I begin to have some sense of my being, of my life, of this stranger within me. I have a connection to myself that has nothing in common with my daily absence of connection with myself. I begin to have what could be called another relationship between these centers of mine. The work is about re-relating, about bringing about a harmonious relationship between the head, the body and the heart. As it is, it's a sort of a ridiculous troika. I don't feel what I think. I don't think what I feel. My body has only its own appetites to be served: its impulses to sleep, to eat, to hank and pank.

Mrs. Welch:
But they can have a relationship. Don't terrify everybody.

Dr. Welch:
I don't think this is terrifying to anybody. I think everybody in this room knows the experience of a harmonious relationship, and it's not because I invented it. It's something that takes place. And in between, one's attention is, more often than not, on its own. And where my attention is, there I am.

DECEMBER 9, 1994

The subtlety of work. Finding a balance in one's life.

First Questioner:

I've had a question for a while, based on some very partial obser-vations. It seems as though all my efforts are very fragmentary. I try one thing on Monday, and on Tuesday I try something else, having forgotten what I was trying on Monday. Wednesday I wake up, and have a little bit of being, and I can find something when I sit, but Thursday it's something else. Well, I'm not sure… all these partial observations, states that fluctuate, different "I"s…

Dr. Welch:

Do you *see* this? Or are you lost in this?

You remind me of what Mme de Salzmann so often said: "I see that I am in pieces." She was not speaking rhetorically, and if one sees that one is fragmented—in pieces, not centered—this means something, doesn't it? It tells one something about self-observa-tion—not a how-to, not a technique, but that self-observation is very exploratory and very difficult. And you remember Gurdjieff himself said, "You try. Not be astounded if you find that you can't, you don't." It seems to me that what one has to understand about self-observation is that, in its real manifestation, it is, as one has often heard, a reflection of another level of being. And one is un-dertaking to acquire this aspect of self-knowledge.

The heart of the matter is not how I recollect that I am frag-mented, but that, at the time, I have great difficulty seeing that fragmentation, instead of being taken by it. There's a long road to something that qualifies as self-observation. At the same time, you have occasionally experienced an inner demand to observe yourself, and you have seen something about your pattern of re-action to this demand. And the pattern of this reaction becomes difficult to separate from the impression that one is very frag-mented. This is because one's attention is vulnerable to being taken away by whatever appears. This is part of the human con-dition. You're not seeing something that is your sin, but you're seeing something that corresponds to how we are. It is a reflec-tion, really, of our inability to be in relation to whatever it is that we mean by a field of attention.

So, I undertake to anchor this attention, recognizing that my real object is a continued impression of myself. This depends on the quality of attention, on the endurance of attention, on the en-gagement of my interest. But I find that what I'm doing is now and then, here and there, taking a stab at it, and seeing that it doesn't come out so well. I don't have a sense of continuity about this that maintains something.

What I see is that the state that I'm in is not consistent with what we call self-observation. But there are times when condi-tions are such that I am open to something that includes a very different impression of myself. Now, I may not see myself as I am waltzing across 33rd Street, presumably going somewhere, but rather when there is a degree of quiet and a degree of engage-ment with this field of attention. And, as you said, *sometimes* I can reach something, and I see that it's not so simple, not so easy. It's very difficult when I'm in motion in life.

When the screws around me tighten up, I don't even recall the necessity. Or I may, but I will explain to myself that I'll try a little later. How do you see a way of continuing to undertake something that you find elusive—to keep on trying? You're not unfamiliar with certain of your patterns of response to life, are you?

Same Person:
No.

Dr. Welch:
This has come about, either directly or indirectly, because some-

body stuck a stick into the spokes, and you saw something. This is a piece of self-knowledge that may not be enlivening or particularly reassuring, but you know something about the little triggers that produce your characteristic way of having a negative attitude toward somebody or something. This knowledge is not without its value, not without its relation to what you're after.

Same Person:
It seems to me that I need some power or some strength, in order for something to take place—to have some being, to know what's real. I don't want to use the word "accomplish," but...

Dr. Welch:
Well, you know, I think everybody's experience with this wish for some aspect of transformation is that, when something takes place, it doesn't seem to be in relation to the work that I've been doing on myself at all. Suddenly, somebody does something, or says something, or there's an occasion when I feel particularly taken by the conditions that I find myself in, and something opens in me. And I'm apt to think, "Well, this is electronic in character. This is not my stubborn climbing over the barricades of myself into some freedom." It wasn't anything like that at all. How does one associate that with this thing that you're visualizing: a kind of linear pursuit of something over all these barricades? But it isn't that.

Same Person:
I wouldn't characterize it that way.

Dr. Welch:
You just did. You said, "I don't want to say 'accomplishment.' What I would like to do is have more being." Well, these are all words that relate to the way in which one undertakes to approach this work. And it's understandable, and it isn't necessarily wrong. One has to do all the wrong things for a long time before one sees that one is on the wrong ladder. The ladder on which I take myself by

the scruff of the neck and, by my assertion, achieve something, is the wrong ladder.

There *is* something called will power. It may be just a fragment of will, but will enters into this. And it's not self-will, and it's not that thing called "grit," but something about an inner recognition of the sense, of the meaning, of what I have to awaken somewhere in myself: the recognition of what my real situation is. Mostly I'm stuck because I can't run my own show. And I see that I'm not running it, but I try to run it. That's not the point. The point is that there is another avenue in myself that is very, very mysterious. But it's not grit and determination, with my teeth set. Do you follow this?

Same Person:
Yes.

Dr. Welch:
It's very subtle, you know. This is not something that one learns to do in the ordinary way. What one tries to be is more and more available to the inner conditions that are *not* related to how I can improve the situation, to how I can manipulate this thing. I need to drop this determined pursuit and let go of all this well-known capacity to conquer in the world. This is what is impinging on me, and I would wish to be relaxed, not tense, not concerned with how I am doing, but rather with how my own inner conditions begin to be more appropriate for the appearance of something that I don't really understand, except, perhaps, theoretically. And it's a mystery. It really is a mystery, because it isn't amenable to my conventional capacity for wrenching what I want out of my environment. I'm trying to allow something to stop repeating in me, to drop this periodic tension that characterizes what I'm doing.

Same Person:
The strength that I spoke about is like a conviction, like a thread, like knowing with a compass which way is north—not forcing something, but so that I don't lose my way.

Dr. Welch:
But we do lose our way.

Same Person:
Yes. That's why I asked my question.

Dr. Welch:
That's why you're here, you know. Because you know very well that you lose your way. But suppose you found your way? Would it last?

Same Person:
I can only hope so.

Dr. Welch:
Yes, but who do you know who has moved up the ladder, and off the ladder, and onto the threshold of God knows what?

Same Person:
Besides yourself?

Dr. Welch:
Oh, sure, sure. [laughter] Have I ever suggested that?

We're all on the side of the same mountain. And some have been hanging around longer than others. And there are a lot of ropes that help, for the most part. And it's terribly important for us to have a sense that *somebody's* getting somewhere. But it always fascinates me when I look at the life of someone like Saint Teresa of Avila. To read her words you would believe her to have been what she asserts herself to be, a terribly unworthy sinner. And the fact of it is that she was a very great human being, according to the requirements of human beings. And it seems to me that if you get to be a great human being, then you *really* see what a mystery you are and how you miss the mark.

But all one needs, at the level at which we work, is just a glint, just a little bit. Whatever one experiences on the way is a taste.

It's not a conversion. It's not a change. It's not a movement. And one doesn't learn overnight. That's why that statement always rings so true: "It's the journey; it's not the destination." As Tracol puts it, "It's a permanent search."

But, what we tend not to appreciate is that on that route we do *see* from time to time. We see what is, from time to time. You've described what is, but rather as you've experienced it, not as you've seen it. It has taken you, rather than your being active in relation to it, and not just reactive. Occasionally you are active in relation to it, but there isn't a complete transformation. One gets a taste of this from time to time.

And I'm not sure that anybody is quite certain that they really want to be transformed. What does it mean? It isn't so easy to say that one has the choice. But curiously, the side effects, the by-products, of this pursuit have a kind of value. One sees that, included in the worldview that a man derives from whatever energies he's apt to put into this work, he doesn't get lighter and less engaged by life, but just possibly he simplifies a little, becomes less solemn and more serious. He becomes less naïve about what he can hope for or anticipate, and perhaps rids himself of some of his illusions. And in the best sense of the word, he is disillusioned without being disappointed or depressed about it, because he is just a little bit nearer—if one could really encompass it—to how things *really* are. *Everything* related to everything else. *Nothing* still. *Always* in movement. Everything constantly changing. And yet we think we live in stability. We think we're permanently how we are.

So, one can be less distressed by what one's efforts seem to be bringing about, and more nearly in touch with the scale of the undertaking, more nearly in touch with the difficulty of this work. You can't exaggerate the difficulty of this work; this is work with a capital "W," which doesn't mean that it has to be all tragedy. It's tragi-comic too. It's either the human dilemma or the human comedy, depending on whether you feel about it, or whether you think about it. You have to do both of these things, and then something close to balance can possibly appear.

Second Questioner:
I'd like to ask about balance. I find that I'm either hyperactive, as if I had two hours of sleep, and was living on coffee, and buzzing all the time, or, on the other hand, it's as if the gravity of the earth is pulling me, so I'm just heavy, slow, sleepy.

Dr. Welch:
Well, by balance, I think what we really mean is either the whole or the partial resolution of our contradictions between these two places of leaden inactivity and agitated manic attitudes. There's somewhere in between, because one needs the juice of the enthusiasm and the sobriety of the pull of gravity. And this is really another way of coming to that thing that Mme de Salzmann put so well, called "the look from above." And one sees that suddenly one is touched by the meaning of the triangle. There's "yes," there's "no," but up here it's covered. It's not so easy to find a place in yourself that can entertain "yes" and "no." It is not something that one does by a determination, but something that can appear in one, in which one sees how partial is "yes," how partial is "no." At the same time, there's something "yes" and there's something "no" about most of our dilemmas, and the essential dilemma—ourselves.

Same Person:
It's as if I'm on a platform and the trains just keep running by, and never stop for me.

Dr. Welch:
Well, it's only true if you're at a local station when there are nothing but express trains. Otherwise, there's always another train. You'd better change your metaphor. What do you mean the train never stops? You have all kinds of opportunities in life.

Mrs. Welch:
If you recognize them. You sometimes don't recognize them when they take place.

Same Person:
Another way of saying it is that I leave myself out.

Dr. Welch:
I doubt that, and so do you. What do you mean, "You leave your-self out?" Your inner self? You just go with your personality? You leave your essence out? Is that what you mean? How can you do that? Do you think you have a golden essence? Maybe it's brass. There's no guarantee that essence is other than what I was born with. What do you mean, "You leave yourself out?"

How do you put yourself *in*? You mean you're never whole?

Same Person:
It's like I'm not participating in my life, like I'm passive.

Dr. Welch:
Yes. You're not alone in that. What does it mean to be whole-hearted? Why are all of us, more often that not, lukewarm? Who is always ready? How can one come to some place where, when the occasion arises, there is something in one that can respond? I think it's related to this thing we were talking about a little while ago. Although linear work cannot be expected to change any-thing, it nonetheless gives you a practiced instrument, which can be more nearly available, because it has been honed—not with the idea of self-improvement, but with the idea of becoming sim-ply less reactive.

There is a reasonable value in working on the quality of at-tention, not because you're going to attend to something that will be "very interesting," but because then the instrument is not un-accustomed to something other than like, dislike, and reaction. So that when conditions change, and circumstances become less blurred, less confusing, one is not quite so jumpy, not quite so smart aleck, not quite so concerned with oneself, but more nearly concerned with what is. One can then become more in touch with this thing that I would call the field of attention, and one cannot then be entirely unaware of how one is. When something is awakened in me that approaches another level, it's not because of what I'm doing, but because of what I'm available to. It goes through me. It isn't something that *I do*. And I can't manipulate things to produce that, but I can become less of a fixed automaton.

After a Movements demonstration the week before.

First Questioner [a musician for the Movements]:
Watching the Movements, night after night, I came to appreciate their incredible design in a way I had never been able to absorb by watching a film. All the different complexities that are built in... Certain things are almost impossible to do, for example, to keep your arm moving in a smooth circle when you are moving around like a wave. But something about the design is very different from watching someone do ice ballet, for instance. There is a perfection and a beauty in that too, but it is a completely different kind of thing. In a way, the impossibility points to something—another world, really.

Dr. Welch:
One thing about the Movements is that very few of them tend to duplicate what we call reflex movements of the body—the coordinated reflexes that are available to a percussion hammer, and so on. There are various ways, it seems to me, in which the reflex movements of the body are deliberately opposed.

Certainly, one has always learned that the Movements were mathematically designed. They have nothing in common with ordinary movement, particularly ordinary movement that is designed to express something. You are at your wit's end to discover what the Movements themselves express.

The more one sees of the Movements, the more one sees that they are not impulsive, but are designed in a subtle, inscrutable way that has an impact that isn't necessarily understandable or definable. But they do something to the emotional center; they do something to the mind; they certainly do something to the body. And one understands something about containment in movement, and something awakens emotionally that one has no way of anticipating, except through the experience of undertaking certain inner efforts. It is a very profound device for self-study, for self-awareness.

Second Questioner:
I think that sometimes I am so focused on my personal reactions, in a strained kind of searching to figure out where I am, that I am missing the mystery of what is moving through me.

A couple of times this week, I have had the sense that I am actually focusing on the completely wrong thing, and that there is something hidden that is happening at the same time as all my little personal stuff. It is separate, but connects us and moves through us, and I am missing it.

Dr. Welch:
It is true and very interesting, what you say. The truth is that everybody has their own little attitude about what they expect, what they are seeing, what they experience. Some are moved; some are not moved; some are swayed; some are not swayed. What you describe so nicely is just that very local little spectrum of personal preoccupations, personal opinions, and personal attitudes—all the things that make us very parochial, very provincial, and not worldly—in the sense of the world of mankind, the world of experience. It is very interesting to see that. It isn't so much that one is concentrated on the wrong thing. The wrong thing belongs there, too. But one is not concentrated on the right thing. It is very interesting, particularly if one sees that this is one's pattern of seeing, of experiencing, of participating.

Third Questioner [a participant in the Movements demonstration]:
I have been reluctant to speak about the 13th because I feel so far away from it. I feel baffled by the contrast between the strength

of the feeling that was evoked for me during the whole preparation and the question "Where does it go?"

In the work before the 13th, on January 2nd, so many of the
Movements were still not yet known, really. I remember Paul
[Reynard] saying, "Well, the 13th is ten days away, and we don't
know what that will be, and the opportunity is now." In a way,
day by day, it was like that. The opportunity was now. I felt able,
for the first time ever, to keep putting the emphasis on the inner
work. The work itself came first, in a way.

At times during the preparation, and on the 13th itself, the
idea became very clear that we were not demonstrating anything; we were not expressing anything, in the way we usually
think of expressing something. Perhaps something could be expressed, but we were there to discover and to follow something.
And I felt that that was actually mostly true, to the point that,
when I made mistakes, I wasn't devastated, although I felt badly
to disturb the class.

Afterward, listening to the music, the feeling I had was: "Why
can't my attention be stronger? Why couldn't I follow even more?"
But it was very new to me to dare to work at all in front of others while being watched, and not to retreat behind the security
of knowing precisely what follows what, and being completely in
that dimension.

But somewhere around Monday, the feet of clay reappeared.
When we were speaking of what's behind where we all are all
the time—this sense of mystery—I wondered why I don't simply stop. There is always another dimension that is alive. I am
not in touch with it, but I just recently have been, thanks to
these conditions of working every night, and even thanks to the
difficulty of organizing my life to be able to. All of that produced
a very strong demand. It would seem to be enough just to stop,
but I can't.

Dr. Welch:
Do you know why?

Same Person:
At the beginning, it is there with me, and I think it will never leave. When it leaves, I don't dare look, in case I can't find it.

Dr. Welch:
In a way, it is the essence of the work that it does not have momentum by itself. One only finds oneself able to bring that momentum while one is at another place in the relative distance between levels of being, levels of existence. One is not quite anchored in the state of total mechanicality. These varieties of levels of living are not accomplished, but rather something works through one when something in one is available to be worked through. How could one expect not to be in another state with the conditions of the Movements—a kind of celestial road map, for God's sake? The impact of these positions on one is such that one's inner conditions are entirely vivified.

And then there is that observer who says, three days later, "How can I be so indifferent to all this?" I see that everything is in motion; everything changes. And I don't have any relation to all the elements that made up the circumstances of the 13th, and all the days before the 13th. You know, it seems to me that we are faced with the reality that the magnitude of this work is difficult to exaggerate. You know what Gurdjieff said about it? He said, "This no cheap thing." What you are saying is a verification of that.

Same Person:
I suppose the question would be how to be related to changing. How could I be placed differently in relation to it?

Dr. Welch:
One has to see, as has been said in the old days, from time to time, that when you work, work, and know you work; and when you stop, know you stop. The difficulty is that we are always getting mixed up about who is the passenger. And it is not so simple because one is not, so to speak, in charge.

Same Person:

I know that it was a gift—handed to us—but because we worked every evening, there was a whole other quality of life, of quietness. All the absurd things that go on in life continued. Things were topsy-turvy as usual, but there was a different relation to them. It was that as much as the feeling that came when we actually worked on Movements. Something stayed connected, just a little bit, which shed a completely different light on all the absurdities.

Dr. Welch:

The approximation of maintaining an inner connection that's not irrevocable... But there is an echo, a resonance, which one experiences.

FEBRUARY 10, 1995

Why don't I work? Will. Fulfilling one's role.

First Questioner:
I feel guilty that I haven't worked. And right now, it seems to me almost amazing that anything is possible at all. At one point, while sitting earlier this evening, it just became clear to me how much I am centered on myself. It's very, very persuasive that what is going on in me is important, and there is no recognition that there is something else in this world at all. And even recognizing it and seeing the absurdity of it didn't change it right away.

Then, from kind of not denying it, it slowly changed. Or maybe it changed all at once, I don't know, but later it was different. I don't always notice the moment when something changes. Or perhaps I don't recall it. But in the absence of that feeling that comes, it is very hard to work during my ordinary life.

Dr. Welch:
Which says what?

Same Person:
Which says I need help.

Dr. Welch:
Yes, we all need help. And what is help?

Same Person:
At its simplest, being with others so I persist, I think.

Dr. Welch:

As Gurdjieff put it, "We can only provide conditions. We cannot help." And one appreciates conditions, yes? One has the feeling, probably close to remorse, that one has allowed another long stretch of the hours of one's days to pass without awareness. And this is somebody who has been reminded, and helped, and is persuaded that he is serious about this. How can it be that someone, who is almost conditioned to this, finds it difficult to work without something jolting him? He finds that he has no fragment of will; that, even by association, he can't find the place in himself that allows another look on himself, another vibration rate, a recognition of how it is, and how *I am not*. It doesn't say something about your persuasion. It doesn't say something about your wish. It says something about the level of being that we all share.

We share this, but we don't *see* it. You were lamenting your self-preoccupation at a moment when there was an active possibility for attending just to that, yes? This is a difficult experience, because, when one is lost in whatever narcissism goes on in one's inner life, one has to acknowledge that Gurdjieff's description of us is not far from the truth. The difficulty is that we know it in our heads, but we have great difficulty experiencing it for what it is. And somehow this has to do, I think, with the gulf in the space between levels of being.

So, one makes another resolution. How can one turn to some inner discipline that requires a decision? Gurdjieff used to say that the decision to work is much more difficult than to actually work. It's a curious slant. But one can get the taste, the flavor, of this. How does one make a decision that is based on an acknowledgment of need and a sense of the vision of the possibility?

It is clear that many of us are very busy with the business of the Work, and we believe "we are in the Work." In fact, we might just as well have a job at AT&T, because that's the way we go at it. We want to do it very well. Then one sees, perhaps, this curious evasion—not an intelligent evasion, not an articulated evasion— that one is very busy: no time, meetings, all kinds of work, all kinds of business, all kinds of planning, all kinds of "*rrrrrrr.*"

And then one sees that that is what one is doing, and something changes.

When one first hears these ideas they sound eminently sane and hopeful. One remembers the expression "brilliant common sense." Given the circumstances, which don't sound at all unsuitable to one's own experience, what could be more reasonable than to work on oneself?

We don't speak these days as much about conscious labor, intentional suffering, struggle, effort. We don't speak about effort so much now, because we know that often this is strain, and often one is concerned with how one can approach the idea of effort without grinding one's teeth, without tensing one's muscles, without being seized by the determination to accomplish. Gradually, one comes to a place about self-observation that is not so much a microscope looking at a little crawler, but something less tense. And almost all human circumstances, inner and outer, are the occasion for awareness of oneself. Why do we find this so difficult?

We find it difficult in retrospect. Why did I allow that time to pass? Everybody has the same difficulty you brought. How do we deal with this? Or do we? Why is tomorrow like today? If nothing changes today...

Second Questioner:
The form that it has been taking in me is that I find my thought processes constantly revolving around various ego concerns that I don't actually believe in. I find it very odd that much of the time I don't believe in what I'm thinking—hardly at all.

Dr. Welch:
You don't believe that you believe it.

Same Person:
If you like.

Dr. Welch:
I like that a little better than "I don't believe it."

Same Person:

Something in me strongly does not believe it. In the past, I think I was more taken in by much of this. It strikes me as very peculiar and appalling that it goes on nonetheless, and it still has all its power, even though I don't believe it.

Dr. Welch:

You don't believe it with your head.

Same Person:

Right.

Dr. Welch:

I think that that is important, because one doesn't manifest out of one's head. One manifests out of one's midriff, out of one's emotional state, out of the thing that moves us. It is a strange compulsion that moves me. It is very touching, I think, this sense of being seduced by something that one knows is fraudulent, but at the same time, one sees that one's manifestation doesn't deny it.

Same Person:

I agree with you completely. What seems clear, at times, is that there is a whole associative process, which is emotional, which I don't really have much to say about, or even much knowledge of. I certainly don't understand it. It doesn't make a lot of sense. It has the same quality as being addicted to smoking. Something that one knows comes from somewhere else.

There are two ideas that struck me this week, ideas that I have been familiar with, but that previously never struck me as so real. One of them is the idea of the formatory apparatus, which always sort of stuck in my throat. It struck me this week that that is exactly what much of this so-called thought is. It just takes things that are coming from somewhere else entirely, from other places, and turns them into words. It doesn't have anything to do with real mind.

The other one is the idea in yoga, which I just happened to

bump into again, that the seer or the seeing is completely separate—that it is separate from the mind and from what is seen—and that all confusion, human confusion, comes from mixing the seer and what is seen.

Mrs. Welch:
What do you expect to receive from your recognition of this? What is it that you are looking for, so to speak? How will it clarify?

Same Person:
I find both of these ideas clarifying, if I can remember them. At times, I can really perceive this. Something in me sees, and sees everything. It sees my sensation and it sees my thought, and is not any of them. And I can even get a glimpse of falling out of that, by becoming attached to a thought-feeling that comes along and grabs me, and I become identified—that's a perfect word—with it and go off into a level of perception which is clearly less whole.

Dr. Welch:
I'd like to ask a question. What is the role of will in the Work? I am not talking about "free" will. I am not philosophizing about will. But I am asking about whatever fragment of will we may have, because we have some evidence of willing to be, willing to do. What is the role of will in the Work?

What is one's experience with this phenomenon, this capacity in one's ordinary life? Are there any occasions when it played any part? Or was it just like and dislike? Has anybody had the experience of undertaking something quite coolly, and pursuing it, and seeing to it that one didn't allow oneself to lose one's way at mi-fa? Is there any evidence for some responsibility, for some quality of will? Does anybody have something to say about this?

Third Questioner:
I have a little something to say about it, but I am not sure it really qualifies as will.

Dr. Welch:
Well, I think we have to be tentative about these things, and it is right that you should begin from there. I was hoping to begin somewhere near there too. Go on.

Same Person:
The impression I have is that the closest that I come to it is in situations like what happened this evening. I had planned to leave work in time to grab some dinner before I went to the sitting. And I got a last minute phone call, and that made me a few minutes late, and then the subway was jammed up, and I was delayed there. And when I finally got out, near the Foundation, there simply wasn't time to grab dinner. And although I toyed in my mind with trying to grab a slice of pizza on the way, I essentially just said that there was no time, and my stomach had to wait. It's so minor, so trivial in a certain way, but something was able at least to hear that it was important for me to go straight to the Foundation. It felt to me that I could perceive, in that little incident, where will could, one day, enter or grow from—that there could be, in me, the potential to go an extra step when it is called for.

This also seems to relate to a rather odd experience that I think I've had over many, many years of going to Work events of various kinds. It's almost nonexistent, in my experience, that I'm unable to meet that commitment, or to meet that schedule, in the midst of sometimes extremely complex projects coming in at the office, and so forth. Somehow, with great regularity, I can slip out the door, at just the right time, to get where I need to go. Maybe it's just a wish or imagination, but there's almost the sense that that's the closest thing I have to will, and it isn't mine.

Dr. Welch:
I think it's close. I think that this is perhaps where we are, for the most part. We know something about self-will. We know a little about another quality of will. It has something to do with decision, I think. There are conditions in which one is moved to

weigh the possibility of a decision, particularly if one is under an influence that seems to correspond to the hopefulness of this.

I think there is something about reliability, about responsibility, that evokes some aspect of this. Many people know that they have experienced going, with great resistance, to some event and then discovering that that great resistance was not fulfilled, and that something took place that corresponded to what they felt, fundamentally, was the movement within them.

One knows this. But it's very troubling for one to discover that, after a reasonable number of years, one has not found the inevitable circumstance making an effective difference in the way one lives one's life. What happens to this conviction that one says one believes in? What is the role of faith? Does one forget, or is one forgotten? What is it that magnetizes one, and then one is untouched by? What is the work?

Fourth Questioner:

I find the question "What is will?" very difficult, because, although I am considered a relatively responsible person, and all the rest of it, I feel that, in fact, I do what I want to do, and I don't see any hint of something that corresponds to will. Is will considered to be against desire? Or comfort? What is will?

Dr. Welch:

It has been defined in lots of ways, none of them very satisfactory. But all of them relate to some kind of interchange in the mind, in a field that provokes some action, so that there is a weighing and a remembering of a point of view, of a point of application. So, it's not without its struggle. And it isn't always clear what one's need may be, as compared to what one's wish may be. But I certainly don't disagree for a minute with you when you say that it seems that one does what one wants, deeply. And I have difficulty imagining that I am piloting the ship in accordance with real inner demands, or with the presumed destination of the ship.

I think that experiential awakening to my perception of the true nature of my manifestation is very different from my head knowledge that I am mechanical. Because I very quickly persuade myself that I am busy with all kinds of things that are "my work." Therefore, in spite of everything, I am all right, because "I am in the Work."

. . . .

Gurdjieff said a lot of things that were not said lightly, and one remembers them. "Ordinary effort doesn't count. Only super-effort counts." At the place when effort becomes super-effort, it suggests to me, somehow, that this may have an element of will. One cannot speak of this as though one is grandly familiar with it. But only this kind of stretching beyond ordinary effort, as he says, counts. He doesn't leave much space for temporizing, but at the same time, these things are always relative within one's own scale of life. And there are degrees that go in this direction and things that probably don't awaken what is, perhaps, a potential capacity of man. You know, there are lots of arguments about "free will," "Thy will," "my will," "self-will," and so on, but I think it is not something that should be entirely out of one's terrain. There is something that approximates, in one's life, an intentional decision related to an aim that has nothing whatever to do with whether the moment is pleasant or unpleasant. But surely, it is not just a moment of self-control, of self-domination. That's much too close to the narcissistic place of accomplishment, of achievement, of being able to demonstrate that one is tough and unrelenting.

So, we don't find ourselves as masters of this widely weighed capacity of ordinary man, but we do see the absence of intention. We do see the absence of awareness, but not *acutely*. Not *experientially*. We always say, "Well, this morning it was terrible."

. . . .

One realizes that one is only in the Work from time to time. So, the many years that we credit ourselves with require a little pruning, a little grain of salt. We are all "zigzag idiots with five

Fridays a week." How can it be that with a prolonged and conscientious association with a movement that calls itself the Work, and which is imbedded in something called effort, we are haunted by the inner recognition that there are great hiatuses in our serious pursuit of this worldview?

The work is on oneself. It is not easy to determine just exactly what this is, but one experiences something that has a nuance that is far clearer than any kind of self-discipline that might be ordinarily undertaken in the less rigorous world of philosophy, or what have you. We all have this experience of recognizing how little we actually work. We all know this very well.

Somewhere here there is a connection with will. Somewhere here is a connection with decision. Somewhere here is the difference between true inner illumination and saying, "I certainly am very automatic, and I see that I am very automatic." The moment of illumination is difficult to come to, and one can't do it on purpose, but one can have an affirmative attitude that isn't just occupying oneself with the business of the business of the business of the Work. One can have one's own affirmative, active pursuit of the conditions that allow the experience that gives one a taste that brings a wholly new impression of what, in an ordinary way, one would say one already knows all about.

Then one sees the stranger that one doesn't know, and it is not a heavy creation and an overcoming of barriers, so much as it is coming to the place where one really undertakes to work— perhaps not without moments of great help. It's touching and very helpful to hear the music of the Work, the music of the Movements—the mathematics, or whatever the hell it is. It is the forethought of the choreography of the Work, which is waiting for you to move into it in such a way as to provoke an impulse in you that you'd had no intention of. One is helped by the "sly eye" of the forethought of the Movements, and of many otherwise apparently contrived circumstances which appear, and the impact of a great many things that one doesn't have any way of putting on a scale.

Mrs. Welch:
Yet there is an effort to turn to, isn't there?

Dr. Welch:
The taste, yes, the taste of the work.

Mrs. Welch:
It requires an effort of seeing where the movement toward work actually takes place, because self-deception doesn't help.

Dr. Welch:
No, self-deception doesn't help, and undertaking to comprehend the principle is so much more difficult than we imagine. Because we are so imbedded in a texture of what I think cannot be described as other than lies, which are based, not on evil calculation, but on the absence of data, and the confidence of assertion in the absence of data: "I know all about myself." I don't say that, except to myself. "And I mean self-observation. I do that a lot, you know. I often see what a fool I am. It doesn't seem to move me very much."

This is an effort that has some relation to will. It has some relation to a responsibility to something that I half experience and half acknowledge, but which touches an *obligation* that, again, I half acknowledge.

Fifth Questioner:
I found what you have said about these half-acknowledged obligations to be true, particularly in the face of my mother's illness. When she first became ill, I had strong impressions of myself and my relationship with her, and how I know, deeply, what is lacking, and yet I live on in this day-to-day way.

I felt, I would say, a struggle with myself, for an unbearable moment, when she was gravely ill. And I decided to try to carry the question of how to be toward her when I saw her. And as the weeks have passed, day by day, I've seen my emotional demeanor become very ordinary and very petty. I'm looking for an effort that will really fulfill my responsibility, not just control my emotions on the outside, on the surface. But I would say that I can't do that by myself. I go every day, but I don't seem to have it in me to make such an effort. What does it take to have a question and live there?

Dr. Welch:

One can take, as the poet said, a limited dose of reality[1]. To be confronted by the evidences of mortality of one who was your center of gravity from your beginning in life, is a staggering thing to face, no matter how one might be expected to be prepared for it. The depth of that relationship with your mother can't be measured; it goes to the heart of everything that your life has contained up until now.

One finds oneself helpless in the face of making some substantive impact on someone who is, to whatever extent, occupied with the recognition that what was once inevitable is, very likely, now imminent. In the face of mortality one is numb, unless one entertains a certainty of paradise or the other myths that we comfort ourselves with. There is something merciless about this. I think your recognition of being, in a sense, empty, in the face of this, is so much more nearly what is true about us than so many other common ways of responding. One can respond to someone else's death by saying, "Ah, poor me." How absurd. You are not doing that. You are in limbo, perhaps. But you are not missing the experience. The fact that you don't wiseacre about it, and the fact that you haven't got a lot of imaginary things going on about it, is evidence of your being as you are—not in a state of irresponsibility.

What can one do, other than be present as much as one is able? Perhaps only to take the hand of someone who is alone. This is an

---

1   From *Burnt Norton* in *The Four Quartets*, by T. S. Eliot:
    "Go, go, go, said the bird: human kind
    Cannot bear very much reality.
    Time past and time future
    What might have been and what has been
    Point to one end, which is always present."

experience that nobody can avoid, but nobody does it other than alone. Such an experience shocks one into a state of awareness that is very much related to the greatly papered-over inevitability of everybody's birth and everybody's death.

These are ominous mysteries that one *doesn't* understand: where one came from and where one is going. But it isn't something that requires from you, I think, anything other than presence, and as much awareness as you can bring, and the recollection that the one who is going through this is confronting the recognition that this could be the final solitary experience of life.

I think what you didn't emphasize, but what is the most important aspect of the whole thing, is that you are there every day. You bring the history of your life to the source of your life, and nothing has to be superimposed on that. I don't have anything by which to judge this beyond your statement, but it sounds to me so true, and so corresponding to a place in yourself that is appropriately concerned with the seriousness that this experience inevitably contains. And you are fulfilling your role.

How does one prepare? One is not prepared for this, not directly. But your own sense of your own existence is very much present in this. How to be ordinary is not so easy. You know, Gurdjieff used to speak a great deal about the necessity to become ordinary. This is without "pink lemonade." There is something very touching about discovering something that would be, in another light, not as unusual and remarkable as it is—but to be simply participating in something one cannot understand, but that one can be deeply understanding of.

There's a great gulf between the parents of one's childhood—gods and goddesses, you know—and the recognition of their vulnerability and their common shared humanity that one gradually comes to. It gives one a whole new view of the continuity of the roles that we play, without a script, for our lifetime. I am sure that your mother is supported and is the better for your appearance at her side.

Mrs. Welch:
We still have much to learn.

Dr. Welch:
It is a strange thing, the *intensity* of feeling. What in the world is it? Where does it arise? It is one of the great mysteries, you know, that mankind has something that is capable of just mass reflex, but as it refines itself, it is a feeling-perception that is amazingly awake and versatile. And the fact that it moves one is an extraordinary thing, which one understands very little about. But one should be grateful, not just for the intensity, but for the penetration of the mind, because something takes place between the head and the heart.

Mrs. Welch:
The sacred number is three. I think, I feel, I sense. That's what we are, if only we could remember it—not just fall in love with what we think, or what we feel, or what we sense. These are all aspects of being a human being. We have much to learn, but how are we going to learn it as directly as possible? But that's where we are.

Dr. Welch:
Everything changes, doesn't it?

Mrs. Welch:
Brings change, brings understanding, if we will only find our way to being available. We have, "I think, I feel, I act." Do we have, "I understand"? Well, we have moments of it. We have times when we do.

Dr. Welch:
The possibility exists.

Mrs. Welch:
Oh yes, very much.

At a crossroad. Intentional suffering. Resistance.

First Questioner:
I was touched by what was said last week. I feel almost the opposite: that I don't try intentionally, but that I would know how if I did. In a way, I've been guided. Everything happens to me, but I try to live well, to make a good life for my children, and so forth. I suppose that is in the category of serving nature. I go to the Foundation...

Mrs. Welch:
How do you feel now?

Same Person:
That nothing intentional comes from me now.

Dr. Welch:
Has this changed from a time when you were intentional?

Same Person:
I have had times of being more so, of being less swept along and being more able to stop and try.

Dr. Welch:
So, everything is solved? There are no questions?

Same Person:
Well, yes, I always feel as though there's no question. There is the question of trying. And when I try I will have something to bring, some material. But I want to participate.

Dr. Welch:
Well, you have this to bring.

Same Person:
I suppose that what occurs to me as a question is how to look at that? How to see that? Where to be?

Dr. Welch:
When does it occur to you that you have nothing of this kind to speak about?

Same Person:
During the day, before the group.

Dr. Welch:
Well, what does that mean? [pause, with no answer] Does it mean that you are no longer interested?

Same Person:
Well, that's the evidence of action. I wouldn't have said so in theory.

Dr. Welch:
What have you *stopped* doing or trying?

Same Person:
To stop, in the middle of things, and see where I am and what is going on. To see what, at bottom, I wish for, what it would mean to be present—to even ask myself.

Dr. Welch:
Who is it in you who makes this observation that you don't work? Who doesn't work? This is an honest account, because the reason for silence is, more often than not, the absence of some material that relates to something in one's worldview about what is pre-occupying one.

There is a kind of inner convention that there are only certain ways in which one works. And in some sense, one can toe the line, and look at the book, and listen to the voice of Gurdjieff, and remember the admonition of someone who spoke to you. But what is it that impels you? You are at a place where I would be surprised if you were not making some effort right now. This is, in a way, a plea for help, isn't it?

Same Person:
Yes.

Dr. Welch:
Or is it the intonation of resignation?

Same Person:
No.

Dr. Welch:
Your work has always been closer to the Movements than to anything else, hasn't it?

Same Person:
Yes, absolutely. I would say that that is true. But the Movements are a condition that is given, and it seems to me that...

Dr. Welch:
Are there any conditions that aren't given?

Same Person:
I suppose not. But...

Dr. Welch:
Didn't Gurdjieff say, "All we can provide are conditions"?

Same Person:
Well, what about by oneself? Those conditions are given, too, in a sense, but not entirely.

Dr. Welch:

He also said, "Whatever the conditions of your life, these are the best for you." This is the way in life, not in a monastic circumstance. So, without conditions, no work, yes? Without special conditions that I am particularly congenial to?

Same Person:

Something like that.

Dr. Welch:

In which conscious labor is possible? In which voluntary suffering is possible? In which there is the occasion for struggle?

I can't see your face, so I don't know what is going on there.[1]

Mrs. Welch:

I think she's been very open.

Dr. Welch:

It is an interesting... Well, "interesting" isn't the word. It is a kind of crossroad acknowledgment, and one is always at some kind of crossroad. And, you are not naïve enough to make a resolution. You know very well that resolutions are pretty thin broth.

Same Person:

Better than no broth.

Dr. Welch:

But, how do you account for this in yourself? This is not something that none of your peers, none of your friends, doesn't know very well. How do you weigh this? What is your take on this? Do you want to be whipped? Do you want to hire someone to whip you? Do you want to be painted into a corner where you have no possibility of escape?

---

1   Dr. Welch was suffering from macular degeneration, and so his eyesight was very poor in the last few years of his life.

Same Person:
I don't know.

Dr. Welch:
Why did you speak? In order to speak?

Same Person:
In order to participate.

Mrs. Welch:
Of course. I thought from your voice, from the way that you brought it, that you were really troubled in a certain way, and you wished to be clearer about it. What is the origin of that? We always have some idea. Is it a discovery? Or is it a wish to share it? Or is it a hope for help? Because behind all of it there *is* a wish to be more genuine. Why am I interested in what we call, in a rough way, the Work?

Dr. Welch:
What is your interest? Aside from the Movements?

Same Person:
[in tears] It seems as though one has had tastes of there being a different life, and while we are here, being able to be in touch with it.

[Pause while tissues are brought from another room]

Dr. Welch:
Kleenex is the universal panacea. Do you think Mr. Gurdjieff would say those are "crocodile"?

Same Person:
[laughing a bit] Probably.

Dr. Welch:
There is no external obligation. It is only an internal movement.

Many people carry this non-secret with a sense of dismay when it is awakened—a sense of some recognition of the difficulty of arriving, in oneself, at what Gurdjieff called "one's own measure." In the absence of one's own measure, one is susceptible to whatever one interprets as the nature of what one imagines to be others' measuring.

And so the beam in someone's eye, or the indifference, or a movement of one kind or another, is interpreted in terms of my own self-evaluation, which is not clearly... I keep remembering that thing of Gurdjieff's: "You are not what you think you are." How does one come to that? There is something both valid and invalid in this assertion. Because what one, perhaps, is speaking about is some virtuous continuity that one pursues as imagined in someone else. And one doesn't hear the question that is raised, "I try and nothing appears for me."

Same Person:
Yes, I try and nothing appears. As though, because I ask, it should. Of course, one realizes that isn't so, but then there is a kind of lack of courage, or something. Or a kind of fear, because experiences which are genuine and not to be doubted, in memory... Last week Michel [de Salzmann] was speaking about "What can you be sure of?" That was something that stayed with me in the course of daily life, a little bit. But, in the course of my life, some of the things I feel most sure of are some of the impressions I have had through the Work—work with others, not by myself.

So, when I turn to myself and there is an emptiness, I never get further, in a way, than that. I think something should be there just because I turn to look. How does one try? How does one knock on the door and have it not open, but continue to stay there?

Dr. Welch:
This is a question that has concerned this group of people for about three years. And perhaps another way of saying what you are saying is just exactly the thing that we came to, that one turns to oneself and there is nothing there. Where is that inner percep-

tion which can awaken in me, when I can't be in touch with it? When nothing awakens?

And I know very well that I know the difference, and I am distracted by my daily life. I have to say that, instead of staying with the emptiness that I find, I turn away, because there is nothing there. In other words, I don't stay where it is. It is difficult to bear. Or it's boring. Or it's many things. But it's not awakening, because I don't stay there. And I can't say that I *see* my emptiness. I immerse myself in it, if you like.

Same Person:
Yes. That is how I felt when I came. How can I see this? How can one look at that? How can one see?

Dr. Welch:
Well, how can one try? Because already you have judged it: "Oh, there I am, empty. I must be somebody who is just nothing." And yet it has been suggested to me that nothingness is an aspect that I could undertake to be in touch with, in the same way that I can be in touch with not knowing—*not* knowing—without chastising myself, so that I can experience the freedom that can come from being free of these things "I know."

"I know my emptiness." I don't know it at all. I have already judged it, and put it away and have gone about doing something else. But it is suggested that one not be morbid about this, which is what, I'm afraid, one tends to kind of flirt with. And in comes a little self-pity, and in comes, "Oh, what a shame. I once knew something glorious, and now I don't have the force that is required to lift myself onto a place that I know perfectly well." And then I remember that it has been said that "in order to get there you have to be there." "There isn't any way from here to there, but only from there to here."

We know these sly, circuitous ways of tending to thread it through the head, rather than undertaking, at that place, to come into touch with myself by the only "rent in the tent" that Gurdjieff acknowledges.

You can't have a very close, objective experience of your feelings.

Anybody who says they can observe their mind and the flow of thoughts has a lot to explain.

On the other hand, it's possible to remember that attention is one of the great mysteries. I can hear Mme de Salzmann saying, "The work is not sensing your left leg." The work of sensing is to learn to anchor your attention, to learn another quality of attention, to exercise this.

And you know, and I know, that persistence and intensity of sensation of myself brings about, in spite of myself, not necessarily higher mind and the body in connection, but what I have of *my* head and *my* body, in another relationship than there was when I was contemplating my emptiness.

What I need here is not some "spiritual inspiration." I need some interest, interest in the recognition that I don't know very much about this.

I don't care how many times I try it, or in what solemn assemblies I undertake it. I know—inside I know—that it is very, very elusive to get away from my ego, from what I have been told, from finding what they said I would find, from a literal-mindedness—all these things that make my inner life complex and difficult.

But, *that's the way it is*. I didn't expect to turn into an *ange*. And I remember Gurdjieff said that you can't trust your *ange*; you can only trust your devil, because your *ange* is like you, bucking to be *archange*.

Same Person:
When Mme de Salzmann used to say, "Very good is not enough," is that related?

Dr. Welch:
Yes. There is a place where one comes in touch with one's not-knowing. And one comes in touch with that stranger that I *thought* I knew, but never was quiet enough to be in touch with, in another way.

Now, you try this. And the kids holler and kick you in the shins. A pipe bursts. Something burns on the stove. The telephone rings. You say, "Aaagch," or you say, "Well, I tried." You give yourself a little "A" for effort, and go about scrambling the eggs for lunch.

But, you come back. You knew you wouldn't be reprimanded because you know, because you've been around. You are not very different than the rest of us—that is, those that tell the truth.

Same Person:
It is not the feeling of not knowing, it is the feeling of non-being.

Dr. Welch:
Well, you can't have non-being. Being is not transcendence. Being is how we are: distracted, confused, mildly miserable, and more or less content with the dilettante's life, believing that tomorrow it'll be different, when it will be more possible to take advantage of what I really know pretty well anyway, because "I'm in the Work."

Second Questioner:
I find that, when I say I am working, I am always working for a result. Or at least, the momentum, the push, is toward reaching a certain state that I think I remember. And then I am surprised, quite apart from this "effort," that sometimes something awakens that has nothing to do with this guy who is trying something, this guy who thinks he knows that if he sits in the morning, or if he reads this, something will awaken. Something just comes and taps me on the shoulder.

Dr. Welch:
And not necessarily in relation to what you've been trying to do.

Same Person:
Almost never.

Dr. Welch:
It is true that I confuse accomplishment with allowing inner conditions to appear, with making certain efforts that I don't really understand. But at the same time, it can be that something deposits in me, even as a result of a screwed-up, mixed-up discipline that I have heard literally and understood literally.

You know, we are not experts at suspending our preoccupations and coming to a place in which tension is not the chief characteristic of my manifestation, where I shed something. I let go without knowing that I let go, and what I haven't noticed is that from the very moment that I came to another place in myself, I was *very* different than when I was not making any effort to attend to my life.

And it doesn't make a *bit* of difference, this notion of accomplishment. We've said this, over and over, to ourselves. It is the Western notion that you damn well batter down the barriers and proceed, and this isn't so. You can't manipulate yourself into paradise, and you know that. But that doesn't mean that I see that my effort is a manipulation. I don't see that. At the same time, it is not *all* pure anything, and there are streaks of glory in it. Thank God.

Same Person:
That must be the saving grace.

Dr. Welch:
I think so.

Same Person:
This leads me to a question I had this week that I wasn't formulating intentionally, but it just came out of me. Because I felt regret for my manifestations, after the fact, and not necessarily...

Dr. Welch:
[interrupting] Why regret?

Same Person:

Because I felt that there was nothing there. I was gesticulating; I was talking; I was doing what I was doing. There was perhaps nothing good or bad in any objective sense, but there was no residue. There was nobody around, and I didn't even know it at the time.

Dr. Welch:

How do you know it now, if you didn't know it at the time? What good is retrospect? What *is*, *now*, is not retrospect. This is imagination about how you appeared. This is upper class considering, and very little else. *Who* saw what you described? You didn't see it. You have the picture of what was seen.

Same Person:

I agree with you. What you say is correct, but there was a feeling that ultimately evoked the question "Is someone there besides manifestation?"

Dr. Welch:

Let me put it another way. Is there the possibility, at the time, of what we call intentional suffering? What would be true suffering for what I perceive as my inadequate attention, my inadequate presence? What would be a legitimate cause, an occasion for true anguish for the absence of what corresponds to what a man or woman should be?

This is somewhere around the idea of rubbing out those quotation marks. And, if one sees that one doesn't correspond, this is a legitimate basis for organic shame—not social shame, but the recognition that there is something corresponding to the possibility of man that is absent here.

Maybe this is beyond us, but one can be halfway to a true sense of real shame over the fact that one is not the way one would wish to be. And this is, after all, a work that isn't pursuing something angelic, but is just something about human beings who are awake to the approximation of appreciating the obligation that goes with all the gifts that they don't acknowledge.

It certainly is difficult to find, in one's ordinary world of re-action and distraction, where the engagement makes sense. I'm always trying to accomplish some beatific vision or screwed-up spirituality that has a kind of romantic sentimentality about it.

That isn't the point. The point is to see what is possible for a man, for mankind. Because I have enough evidence, over the years, that I have no problem treading the mill, and doing today what I did yesterday, and will do tomorrow. But what do I really see about this, or know about this, or experience about this? I just have a little poetic notion about it: "Oh well, there I am—empty. What a shame." And I would always like not to be empty. I would like to be a sonnet of some kind that would run up and down Ja-cob's ladder and give a feeling of beatitude, because, after all, I have been in the Work for years. Twenty years? Thirty years?

[Speaking to the first questioner] I think you are honest and true, and I am delighted that you have a lot of years ahead of you. It probably is later than either of us thinks, but at least you have got the time.

You know, just because the candle sputters sometimes, it doesn't mean it is going out. In strong winds and in light rains, it can dampen a little, but it can be relighted.

Have we touched anything that helps? Because I don't think for a moment that your experience is fatal, permanent or nec-essarily all that important. One of the things about Gurdjieff's worldview is that, once you get vaccinated, you have a hard time catching anything else.

We get so solemn, you know. It's too bad. It's part of the journey: dry periods, moments of disenchantment, misinterpre-tations, failures to see. But I find that seeing is not so easy. Seeing is very different from being lost in more not-seeing.

....

Third Questioner:
I feel a sense of responsibility to others in the group that I don't usually feel in ordinary life toward strangers or people in busi-

ness. There is the responsibility of offering something, if it is possible, which partially reflects what the person who spoke before me said. It deepens my awareness of myself, for a moment. And that is something that *happens.*

Dr. Welch:
Everything happens.

Same Person:
What I meant to say is that I don't provide the impetus for it.

Dr. Welch:
You mean that this is something that you realize takes place without your intention necessarily being directly involved. And this is very close to the question of accomplishment, the idea of which I do not lose without reluctance. It is very difficult for me to participate in something where I am told that I can't do it and yet it has to take place in me.

Same Person:
Clearly, I don't provide the impetus for what I am describing.

Dr. Welch:
It is not so clear. Because I've had lots of good ideas—I am a fountain of them—and intentions, and resolutions, and dreams. We are bad about that, and there is no use pretending we aren't. Nor is there any point in overwhelming ourselves because it is true. It is just a fact. It is how we are: not unified and not purely motivated. I am in more than one world. And there's no use imagining that I don't turn to the everyday world with relief, sometimes— often with pleasure.

And I am not excluded, nor do I wish to be excluded, from the everyday world. Please notice that I don't say "ordinary life." Because life is not so damned ordinary as I like to pretend. It is extraordinary. It's what I know best, and I haven't found it without riches, great nourishment and people who stand tall. But that doesn't change the capacity to verify the nature of the quality of reaction and distraction. Nothing initiates here. Or very little does.

And in the outside world, in the everyday world, there are these examples that look very close to being related in an inner way, with a hierarchy that is in charge. Whether it is right or wrong, or whether it initiates or not, it has a kind of unity, a kind of ordered thought.

And don't imagine that the only one who ever touched on this was Gurdjieff, because there are many ways to become. I don't think one can be certain that one knows all, by any means, about these ideas.

One forgets that Gurdjieff used to meet certain people, and he would tip his hat and say, "You one in ten thousand." What did he mean by this?

He would also tip his hat and say, "Good night, all kinds." That might be at the door of a restaurant.

Try not to lose the elevation that can come with the extraordinary insight of Gurdjieff, but also try not to be naïve, believing that therefore one is special, and that no one else knows. That's absurd.

The idea of discovering one's nullity and saying, "Oh well, hell, there's no use. I can't do anything about that"...

[Speaking to the first questioner] That is really a way of seeing what you are saying, isn't it?

Now here is somebody who has been exposed to the ideas of the Work for a long time. Among the things that she has heard and has presumably digested is whatever it is that Gurdjieff means by nullity. And I turn to myself, and—hell—there aren't any fires burning. And I am put off. But, I have at least raised the possibility of verifying the level of being on which I live. Is that not so? That's not out of the range of points of reference, is it? And I have to say that my notion of work is to try to turn to myself. So, I have not found something comforting and reassuring on this turn.

And instead of undertaking to be something, in relation to this, other than just being depressed, or in a state of: "That's all there is, and I really must be getting about my other affairs, because there it is," I don't do anything. I don't make any efforts.

This is a very sly kind of resistance. There are those who would say, "Well, you know, demons are very clever with resistance." But, of course, those of us who come from the Western world wouldn't be so sure.

You have certainly participated in this meeting. I think you have broken a wonderful egg. It is absolutely right to bring that kind of reality. Because it has all the network of resistance.

First Questioner:
[The questioner described her relationship with the workmen who were renovating her apartment, then she summarized.] And so, there's been a tremendous amount of considering: "What will they think if I say no? What will they think if I ask for this?" And it's been a steady stream of this, with reactions around each of them. And I've seen this rolling by me, through me, all week. But that seeing doesn't really seem...

Dr. Welch:
...to do very much.

Same Person:
To do anything. I would even say it is almost of the same quality as the reaction. It is an observation, but it's not at any sort of re-move from the experience.

Dr. Welch:
It's after the fact.

Same Person:
So, I guess my question is what, if anything, is possible, is avail-able, in the midst of such a steady stream.

Dr. Welch:
This question of considering is near the heart of the matter. We are capable of so little, other than allowing this evidence of slavery, in a sense. That, in turn, says two things: first, I have no measure of

myself and second, I imagine how I am being measured by others. These are aspects of myself that are characteristic of a certain level of being. There is nobody, with very rare exceptions, who doesn't find this recurring evidence of inner inadequacy. And it is rooted in just this absurdity of my image of myself.

There's only one possibility, aside from really waking up. It's possible, when one is available to oneself in a circumstance in which one is being eaten up by this ridiculous self-deconstruction that goes on with the process of whatever the pattern of what one's considering may be...[A baby in the room fusses and cries]...and it doesn't help any to weep, [laughter] but sometimes we feel like that.

I feel that we're sharing our common experience, not that there is some instruction. My own experience is that it *is* possible—not for long, but in the midst of such an event, when there is a recognition of what it is that is making me suffer—to move, not miraculously, but to move from a kind of resignation of recognition that this reflects *how I am*. And it's only from a place above this that I can be free of this. But if I just want to be free of it, it's very difficult, because it doesn't really work.

Can I move myself internally to a place where the seeing of myself is not the end of what I do, but is the means that I take to come to my best objectivity? Now, how can one undertake this, except in the privacy of one's aloneness? Well, it's not so simple, and perhaps it's not *yet* changing the direction of the energy that is wasted by my simplistic emotional imagination. I accept, and I suspect you do as well, that this is not something new. It just seems...

[The baby interrupts again and there is a pause.]

Dr. Welch continues:
There is something so sort of sobering to be faced with the reality that my suffering is wasted, really wasted. It's the wasted stuff of my life. It puts the whole thing on a level that is anywhere but where I think I am. I can no longer think I am *someone*. At that place, I see the absence of the clarity of my vision of myself.

But I *can* come to a place where I accept this aspect of myself as one of the crowd—a bully, a fragile bully—but there are others of me. There's another side, maybe my best side, that I can undertake to turn to, not in order to imagine that I'm going to rid myself of these parts of myself, but rather because there is another vision in me that can be awakened. It doesn't undo anything, but rather refreshes me and brings me to a place that is less devastating and less absurd. I'm not one. I'm not two. I'm many "ones" and maybe a "pre-flight two." Does that make any sense from your own experience?

Same Person:
Yes, in several ways. One thing is that I realize, with some of these events that took place, that I really do have an image of myself as easy-going, or able to be relaxed about certain kinds of things. And I was really stunned to see how far that was from the truth, how utterly enslaved I was by these worries and concerns and preoccupations.

And there was one incident that was so absurd that it was actually humorous to see how ridiculous my reactions had been. I had written a letter of recommendation for someone, and I had given her a copy, because I thought it would be a nice thing for her to see. And it had been a very good, strong letter. And I didn't hear from her for about a week, and by the end of the week I thought, "Oh, my God, maybe it was not a good letter. Maybe she was furious at me; maybe it wasn't good enough." Then she called and left a message for me that it had been an extraordinary letter, and she was xeroxing copies for her mother and her mother-in-law, and that every time she read it, it brought her to tears. And then I said to my husband, "I knew that letter deserved a phone call."

The whole thing was so absurd, from start to finish, that I actually saw myself, over the course of this week, and at the end of it, just completely wrapped around my own finger. And that was just one of many little encounters of the week. But it was the only one where I actually had even just a second of perspective about how absurd it was.

Dr. Welch:

Yes, it's really a measure of our capacity to be serious. It takes this kind of logical absurdity to make one blink, and say, "For heaven's sake, is it this bad?" And the rest of the time one is wasting the hours of one's days on these imaginary preoccupations that have to do, somehow, with the maintenance of an image, the massage of a fractured ego. As time passes, one sees that this is not something that disappears; it only has large areas where one is indifferent. One can take that to be an absence of considering, but it isn't.

But, despite its endurance, the power of considering to sustain something does have less of an impact on one as time passes. And there is a true monitor, in a way, that comes to one's rescue: the effort that can be summoned, while it's going on, to see it from a different place in oneself. And it isn't a question of causing it to disappear, but causing it to be seen for what it is—to see oneself for what one is.

Same Person:

I guess what I find vexing, in a way, is that it's usually afterward, and often in a situation like a meeting, when I even remember that a look, another look, is possible. In the middle of it, I'm so in love with it, and involved, and carried by it that... I mean that's really my question. Or I don't even know if it's a question. I think I'm just seeing the power of it.

Dr. Welch:

Well, it's not something that one directly reforms. But I think to see the power of it is to see where one really is in relation to being. I think one can realize that this is just one of the characteristics of man at a level of "is-ness" that is not that of a spiritual warrior, not that of a "man without quotation marks." He's just not there.

And I think it's interesting that one doesn't remember. One doesn't remember what we'll just call "the look from above." But it's quite different if one has ever undertaken this gesture of whatever fragment of will we have, and then experienced the freedom that stayed, not forever, by any means, and not for long—I speak for myself—not for long. But it's unmistakable. And one is not only free of the state that one was in, but free of the imagination that one had cured it. One can experience a kind of freedom, which is really freedom from fear, and a lift of the mood to one that is almost joyful. And then, perhaps, the return is inevitable.

But at the same time, that experience is one of hope that, at least, one can—if not deliver oneself from this state—know that there is another place for one's center of gravity other than just in that "pool." One has to suffer, almost more than one wishes, in order to come to that place. But there is somebody in you that knows, right along, that this is the same old record that plays whenever its button is pushed. One sees the pattern of this. It's a terrible damn thing.

Same Person:
You help me remember.

Dr. Welch:
Good.

I think that anyone who pretends that this is something they're free of—assuming that they're conscientious—hasn't really looked. Because we're very clever, you know. We can substitute "principle" for "considering," except that the more we examine the principle, the more it gets wobbly, and considering is there, just a few layers down. It's strange that we are so vulnerable to this.

Second Questioner:
I think I have a question that is connected to this. Tonight I went to the sitting from a somewhat distant place in myself and, despite struggling in various automatic ways, found myself unable to come to a connection with myself, as I had wished. Then, while I was walking up from the Foundation, there was a moment when I admitted to myself that, "I can't do this, and I don't know how to do this, and I don't know how to try." There was sort of a simple

honesty about this fact. And it brought with it a sense of relief. A burden was lifted off of my shoulders.

I wonder whether I'm too glib about these things when this kind of thing happens where I don't feel shame. I forgive myself almost instantly.

But nevertheless there was a sense of relief. I would almost say that the sun came out inside. And there followed something like a sense of humility. I never really found a use for that word in my descriptions of myself, but there was something about this where there was kind of a true, humble recognition that this is the way I am. And some of that came with me into the meeting. And hearing this discussion about considering, there was a little bit of me that was still able to say, sort of, "Yeah, I'm not in control of these things, and I'm quickly prone to considering again." And for some reason the stigma wasn't quite there about this. It's interesting to start to feel this contrast between the way I organize myself around trying not to be this way...

Dr. Welch:
[interrupting] Who in you is speaking? Who sees all this?

Same Person:
I'm not sure.

Dr. Welch:
Very good.

Same Person:
It seems as if the self who sees this doesn't have a capital "S." It isn't a big "I." It's a little "I." But the relief still felt real. There's a sense that there is in me, percolating back there somewhere, a real something. And I caught a glimpse of it—really out of the corner of my eye. It felt almost bigger, in a way, than I even have a right to speak about. It was a little bit more distant than usual, and less connected, but there is a sense that there is something in me that is quite central. The word "being" seems to associate

with it. But it's far off and back in me somehow—it's a metaphor, I think, but... So, I don't know who in me is...

Dr. Welch:
Fair enough. I think there can be an unobstructed, non-considering view. One can be touched by one's nothingness in the right way. In a sense, one comes out from under all that imaginary knowledge, wisdom, capacity, and need to accomplish. One is no longer burdened by this self-illusion for a period, and one feels free. One feels that there's a subtler aspect to this, where one really can come to a place where recognizing not-knowing isn't a critical "Shame on you." Rather, it's a recognition that *au fond* one does not know, and one does not know what it is that one does not know. This is a place from which one can begin, not a place where one signs one's defeat. It isn't defeat. It's more nearly close to a recognition of what one is—not with regard to functioning, but from the subtle point view of another level of perception. Is that clear to you?

Same Person:
Yes, it is. But I also want to ask a question about my strivings in this direction. Varieties of experience do occur, but they feel, in light of all of this, a little bit confused. Connections, if that word makes sense, do occur, but there's a heaviness to *me*, connected with all this baggage that I bring. I have been fortunate enough to experience some change in state, but I'm still burdening it with all sorts of illusions about the process. So, I have this contrast in me, and I can almost feel the movement between being more cloudy or less cloudy. And that's a new perception that actually there's a lot of baggage there that I didn't even realize was baggage.

Dr. Welch:
And you expected the continuity of a direct sequence of accomplishments. Having already even denied that to yourself, nevertheless this is what you expect. You see that there is no direct accumulation of such substantive accomplishments. It's not

the shortest distance, and you have had, in the past, certain electronic experiences, momentary periods of illumination that don't last. And the state in which you found yourself is even difficult to recall. Being ultimately concerned with what it means to be available to another influence is far subtler than I ever remember. This is *not* a predictable, sequential certainty. It isn't. And one knows this because at high noon, on a brisk, sunny day, on the way somewhere to—as I believe we now call it—"do" lunch, it's a little difficult to be sure that one is the same person that went to the sitting and failed, from his point of view.

It's a very meaningful experience, not at all associated with the triumphant warrior of the spirit, but more nearly the reality of all mankind, sometimes, and with many, all the time. It's not necessarily the exception or the permanent reality, but what did you expect? Did you expect to go in and quietly levitate? "I'm going to do my ritual, and watch me rise." No, one doesn't put it that way, but is that what one thinks? Without articulating it?

Same Person:
Something in me has that view, I think.

Dr. Welch:
Sure. We trivialize everything in one way or another. And that doesn't mean that's the only thing we do. But we have many sides. And we don't know them all, by any means. And they're so familiar we don't recognize them. It's an experience of oneself that, in a way, says, "Do you understand a little better that you're not who you think you are?"

Again, self-knowledge is not so easy. Indeed, we're not entirely certain, all the time, what we even mean by self-knowledge. Over a reasonable lifetime, we learn a lot of things about ourselves. But most of them are not quite as they really are, and are only a dim view of a pattern of behavior, a dim view with a quality of "sometimes." But it is not knowing how I am now. Now is a very difficult period because it's in motion. How long is now, if we're talking about linear time and not something that is timeless? And I think we have to be pretty careful while talking about timelessness. It's never something that one has certainty about—or when one has certainty, it doesn't last. The inner conditions that make it possible to be in touch with something that is beyond linear time are not understood. At the same time, one can be illuminated by something that seems to have that essential kind of vibration—not the usual vibration that one is familiar with.

First Questioner:
I have the illusion that I'm in control, or that I can control what goes on in my life. And it seems that what is necessary is some kind of letting go.

Dr. Welch:
Letting go of what?

Same Person:
Of my fear, of my idea, of my preconceived notion.

Dr. Welch:
Your preoccupation, yes?
    And what stands in the way of your letting go?

Same Person:
A fear.

Dr. Welch:
Yes, and fear of what?

Same Person:
I don't know!

Dr. Welch:
Yes, you do. And if you don't know, then it's possible to examine that fear from where you are. To really hug that fear. And try to see where it leads. What *is it* that is making you fearful? And don't tell

me that you can't. You can *observe* that fear. Of course it's an effort, but it's far better to examine that fear and to try to understand where it's from and where it goes. And what is it? And how habitual is it? How well do you know it? Probably very well, because it's been there for a long time, and it appears, and it takes you.

Now when it takes you, you're taken. What can you do about that? How can you withdraw from this, to *see* where it is, what it *really* consists of? And then your attention will wander, and you'll turn to something else, and then you'll come back. And there isn't any art to this, but there is the capacity for attention, however limited. You can try to understand, rather than just to be frightened—just to attend to this, to understand what it is that's moving you into fear.

Now, I don't say you're going to find out for sure, but you're going to have a very different experience of it if you insist on undertaking to examine that fear. Not to try to get rid of it, or to pretend it isn't there, or say, "Oh, hell, it doesn't count." Just to see. Not to become man number forty-two, but just in order to become more acquainted with this fear. To undertake, however difficult that may be, to get a real look at it. Not just to react to it, or to escape it. To stay with it and see it. Not because something wonderful is going to happen, but because you don't know it. And how can you let go of something that you haven't really seen?

Same Person:
That seems to be my question. I'm one step removed.

Dr. Welch:
You may be ten steps removed. It doesn't make any difference how you count the steps. The important thing is, are you able to attend to this? And *really* see what it is? Everybody has the possibility of experiencing what is often talked about as existential fear. If you're really aware of the ambiguity of where you're from, and the ambiguity of where you're going, and the ambiguity of your meaning, and the sense, in any event, of being on a tightrope, it's possible that existential fear will find its way through many

levels in you. It's something to come to know, not with the idea of conquering it at one bout at this, but to undertake to be present to this fear, rather than being in a state of reaction to it.

Do you hear me?

Same Person:
Yes.

Dr. Welch:
Try it.

Everybody in this room, including me, all of us together, to one degree or another, knows how fear enters our lives. This is something that is characteristic, and it is as if it were waiting in the wings. Not always, but when it appears, its sour taste is well known, even to the little boy or the little girl that many years ago first was frightened and didn't know why. We don't live on a level of awareness, but when we undertake to be more aware—because we're shaken by this—there can be another experience of it, if nothing else. And one can be less driven by it and closer to the possibility of coming to a recognition. There is a way of finding the conditions in oneself when one is more nearly in touch with what it is.

Of course, we all pretend that we never have this. But let's not pretend. Let's try to be active toward it, not to destroy it, but to clarify what is going on: to know yourself a little less vaguely. Does this touch anybody?

Second Questioner:
It's the same question I was going to ask.

Dr. Welch:
Is it? Does that help at all? You've tried this?

Same Person:
Well, I don't know if I've tried it. I certainly know that I spend most of my time really trying to escape it.

Dr. Welch:
It's a perfectly understandable thing, and then one sees this. And it's very interesting to take it to where it festers.

Same Person:
We spoke last week about the structure of fear—that it's more important to see the structure of fear than the particular manifestation.

Dr. Welch:
There are so many ways... This subtle thing has to do, in a way, with one's private identity.

Same Person:
Well, the one that gets me all the time is one of Gurdjieff's big three identifications, or whatever he called them—money, stomach, and sex.

Dr. Welch:
[laughing] I always thought that simplified so much. I must say it's not sophisticated psychology. Stomach first, sex...

Same Person:
But money, especially, for me.

Dr. Welch:
And money is the big devil.

Same Person:
It's a real devil, because it's little things that always get me, such as this ticket that I was telling you about earlier. It really is penny-wise and pound-foolish to get in a great state of anxiety about one's future from a fifty dollar parking ticket. And, in fact, it's insidious, because I found the thing on my windshield and there wasn't any real reaction. But then imagination entered. It's almost as if I allowed this to come back, again and again, and bring

out anxiety and fear. And as you said, I don't really see it very clearly. So then, for the next couple of days, that's the dominant tone of my life. There's this slavery to this worry about the future, and all the other things I have to "do," and so on and so forth—imagining that I'm not going to be capable of managing all this.

The mystery to me—and I suppose it's what you were just talking about—is seeing it deeper than just the imagination of the future. I know, as a counter experience, that, after a strong experience in the Work, there is a real freedom from fear that has to do with something much deeper.

Dr. Welch:
Yes, it's a strange thing that our starting point is so provincial, so petty, so close to the ridiculous, and really not that threatening. The great threat is from scale, not from our agitation over a bad report card or being reprimanded for bad behavior. These threats take many forms, and one's emotional life is not grown up. These are remnants of when "God Almighty," who went way up to there [gesturing above his head], said, "You're a bad boy." The reception of this was without any recollection, or knowledge, or insight, but only that one was punched right here [in the mid-section], not up here [in the head]. It may not have been precisely that, but it was the idea of some kind of free-floating sense of not measuring up, of not being welcomed, of not being able.

. . . .

There is a quality of awareness that isn't lost in fear, and doesn't try to push fear away, but rather accepts it. This awareness is not the whole "look from above," but it's far less an occasion for confronting yourself than it is for trying to see it. You're not trying to modify yourself. What you're trying to do is live with yourself—not to pretend that the fear doesn't exist, but to be with it. Now certainly, it isn't true objectivity, but it's in that direction. And one doesn't have a "how to" about this. I always like the expression of just "hugging it."

But if one is haunted by fear, then the question should be: "What is this, really? Where does it go? What is the end point of this? What am I doing with this?" Because I see that I don't wish it, that I'm not in it, but I see that I'm taken by it. The impulse to put it away, to push it aside, to get away from it, doesn't work. It has a beginning, a middle, and it has an end, and it will go away. But it's not unreasonable to undertake to really know it—which is not the same thing as being smothered by it—because one sees that a real attack of this is not a small thing.

Third Questioner:
I can't get away from it in any case. I just make believe I can.

Dr. Welch:
Do you know what you're trying to get away from?

Same Person:
Well, I think it's tearing at the fabric of my self-image.

Dr. Welch:
Yes. But what is it that is tearing at the self-image? What is fear?

Same Person:
I can't say what I think it is, except I think of it as an electric current. I think of it as a current that passes through life and is there, like the air.

Dr. Welch:
Do you think it's wrong to become very simple about this? That it's an absence of force, a perceived absence of force, to meet something that is coming toward me, that threatens me, and that I will be put down by this? I won't find the force I need to deal with this, and I will be thrown into outer darkness for my inability.

Same Person:
Yes, there is anticipation of being overwhelmed.

Dr. Welch:

I think it's an interesting thing, which isn't complicated. One can examine this threat. One can be more nearly an observer of this, at the same time that one is pushed around by it. But the idea of coming to know it, and to see that, my God, the root of this is, among other things, considering, isn't it? Because I see myself as an *observed* victim tossed into outer darkness.

There is lots of innuendo about this, but at the same time, if self-knowledge is accepted as being of some use, this is an aspect of self-knowledge. One can bring what presence one has to it, particularly in these circumstances.

Same Person:

I think, also, that the experience of being thrown into outer darkness actually happens. I'll meet a person, and I'll act like a jerk, and they'll know what a jerk I am, and then I feel the burning shame. And I feel the fear, and I feel terrible, and I recognize that I can survive that also. So, some experience of that is really not so bad.

Dr. Welch:

Exactly. This is one of the things that can be, perhaps, even rightly anticipated in undertaking to see just exactly what it is that has the knife edge of fear for me. What is this? And one does not necessarily come to sweeping generalizations that undo everything, but one does become less unfamiliar with what the unnamed terror really is. Because the terror itself is not articulated at the moment, but there it is.

People were certainly not afraid in that same way in the presence of Gurdjieff. He used to say, "Here fleas don't bite." Certainly not in the same way, because one's fears are really fleabites. There are damn few people who meet a lion in the street...at least not on 84th Street.

First Questioner:

My difficulty is that I'm afraid I'm going to miss something, that somehow there's something going on, and I'll miss it. And I'm so afraid of it that that's exactly what happens. I'm not there.

Dr. Welch:

You know, we haven't been speaking in conundrums. We've really been speaking of our experience. If I were to say, "Repeat the entire conversation as it appeared from each one of the people who spoke," this would be an unfair question. For anybody. Because one certainly was attending, and then not attending, and having associations in oneself that went away from what was being said. And then one went off in something that occurred by association, and then one comes back, and then somebody else speaks, and the same thing takes place. So, it's not a detailed, sequential, instructive account of "how to." It's not that at all. There is no "how to." But each person approached, and drew back, and drew in, and drew back, and then circled, and then clarified for themselves, and for all of us, because everyone's observation is something that one recognizes. One knows something, and one doesn't come away with an answer, but one does come to a place where there is less vagueness and more precision.

And there is not going to be a splendid portrait, but there will be sketches here and sketches there, and the recollection that this is something that's shared widely by mankind, not something that is my personal, particular sin. And we haven't forgotten that the view that we take is that these are reflections of the level of being that we occupy. And there is a certain recognition that it's not as intentional an account as we would like. But we have as a common goal a widening and an increase in what we are pleased to call self-knowledge. We are not unfamiliar with the subject that has occupied us, and we have our experience, and we know we don't control this or anything else very much. But there is the possibility of there being more nearly a "look from above," more nearly a place where there is insight and not just inner confusion.

NOVEMBER 10, 1995
Attitude. Common sense. A continuing exploration.
"You can't do it, but you must try."

First Questioner:

I am a bit familiar with the part of me that judges, that weighs, that keeps accounts, that decides yes or no. I know it's been there for a long time, in the middle of the room just as you come in the door. I don't necessarily want to move it, but I'd like to walk around it, or maybe shift it to the side. I would like it not to be my only experience of my life. But I don't feel particularly like I have to hack away at it, or that I even truly want to be rid of it, because it's often quite useful for sorting things out.

Dr. Welch:

Why do we always want to be rid of something, instead of seeing it? Don't you think this is something we do with considering, something we do with any of the junk that we call our emotional life that is unpleasant? We see a beam in someone's eye, we find ourselves envious or irritated, or feel that nobody gives me my due, and so on. This is the kind of bookkeeper you're talking about, yes?

You don't approve of her, is that it?

Same Person:

I don't know what it would be like if I didn't rely on her so entirely, if I didn't always scurry back to her. The occasions that suggest that there might be something else occur infrequently, and are not easy to grasp.

Dr. Welch:
You know, I think it's a curious thing that this aspect of ourselves is rooted in an attitude, isn't it? And the attitude is that I'm a good judge, that what I see is real, is true. I have my mind made up about everybody. And instead of listening to them, I have my comments on what they say. What does this attitude emerge from? I don't think I have such an attitude, but I come to a meeting like this, and if I don't really remember why I came, I come with my mind all made up about everybody. There are those I approve of, those I disapprove of, those whose faces I know whom I don't really know at all. And I have a little bookkeeper that keeps records of all of it.

That's a nice expression, "keeping accounts." I always liked that. Last year's grudge—keep that account with a little bottom line on it.

You know, the question of reform is always with us. There's more and more talk these days about transformation, not reformation. And yet, we're very close to the reform movement, don't you think? We want to look better inside and manifest better on the outside for all the wrong reasons.

Same Person:
When it's disturbed—this sense that I know what's going on—there's quite a hunger for this other thing that appears. And *then* I can say I'm not interested in reformation. The rest of the time I'm keeping accounts on myself, so that's *all* I'm interested in.

Dr. Welch:
And it's not by intention, but rather some kind of habituation.

Same Person:
I think it's very expensive.

Dr. Welch:
Like free association, you mean? [laughter]

Same Person:
Yes, I do.

Dr. Welch:
"I'm so free!"

It's a waste of time, and it's a lot of things that I haven't really plumbed. But I think it's a clue to that mysterious thing that is an attitude. I'm usually not responsible for having carefully arranged my attitude. It is something that is so much my view of things that I don't notice it. It's like the frame on the picture, and I'm the picture. I don't notice the frame. I don't notice what it is that encloses me and limits me. It's how my more or less familiar turning thoughts carry on. And there must be some sort of trust there that I don't usually weigh, a trust in my capacity to assess—myself, things, people, everything. And how do I get that way? What is the attitude from which this is born? I don't think one answers this so much as one undertakes to approach it from another place. Why am I here?

Mrs. Welch:
When you say "here," do you mean, why am I at a meeting?

Dr. Welch:
Yes, for example. Or wherever I am, but that question is from another place in myself, yes?

Do I have an attitude? Is that fair to say that I come in with my values all arranged? Do I remember what I wish? Am I to accept my persona's entertaining me with all this bookkeeping, all this note taking, all these observations?

I think this is the place for self-knowledge, and not for self-judgment. How does one undertake to be active and present in the mode that I see I've taken? Because I gather it is clear to you that this is something that is a returning persona. It's my *modus operandi.*

It's interesting. I can make an effort to see it, rather than to argue with it, or to make plans to dispose of it. But I find that I don't know enough about self-observation. This is one of those things that I have an attitude about: "I know all about it." Except that real self-observation is, as we often say, a reflection of another level of being. And what we try we drop too soon.

Many people who have pursued this worldview of Gurdjieff discover, after many years, that self-observation is not what they thought it was. They learn that it's much larger, much more difficult, and much less enduring than they thought.

Does that make any sense to you?

Same Person:
Yes.

Dr. Welch:
It does to me, somehow. We all have this question; this is not yours alone. Our attitude is a kind of mystery, really. Because it seems to us that our view of the world is exactly the way things are. But it's our attitude, really. Instead we think that it's the reality of life.

Same Person:
When I try without a presupposition, when I catch myself available, there is so little there, that I do drop it.

Dr. Welch:
Do you stay with that emptiness?

Same Person:
I think I do, and then I wake up sometime later.

Dr. Welch:
Yes. Out "discovering America." It's one of the realities of the fragility of attention, isn't it? It shows me something about my capacity to endure, particularly to endure my own emptiness. I expected to find the pot of gold, but it's not there.

Same Person:
Well, there has even come to be an acceptance that it is going to be empty. Maybe this is just a new judgment that fits in the pattern, and I'll hang it on the tree, but...

Dr. Welch:
Empty of what?

Same Person:
It's very uphill, Dr. Welch. [laughing]

Dr. Welch:
OK. But that's the question, nevertheless. Though it's not a question to be facile with. Neither one of us can be facile with that.

It's a complicated thing to have a good head. You know, you've got a good head; your capacity to cerebrate is not just nothing. It's a provoker, but it has to be marshaled and seen, because sometimes it stands in your way.

Same Person:
By enduring?

Dr. Welch:
Yes, I think something like that. Not a gloomy, solemn, heavy *mea culpa*. But, yes, enduring.

The emptiness has more character than you think, maybe.

Dealing with one's solitariness is something, isn't it? One isn't as alone as one thinks. But that aloneness is not loneliness; it's something else. One is alone *from* something and *from* others, and so on. I don't mean something sentimental about this, but one can awaken to this sense of aloneness.

It's very hard to come to the recognition of a manifestation of the human condition of which I am an example, not a crown prince. I'm an example of the level of being that is the empty automaton, but who has other wishes as well.

Where is that wish? What stands in its way? Does the book-keeper stand in the way of that wish? It's much easier to keep books than it is to remember.

And under different conditions, that isn't the difficulty. One is no longer alone. One shares, and one sees possibility, and maybe hope.

The difficulty is to find the place in oneself that begins to be a little bit "from above." And that means an inner connection, doesn't it?

Mrs. Welch:
Are you implying that one sees its origin more clearly?

Dr. Welch:
Yes, I think so, in a way. But it varies, doesn't it?

Mrs. Welch:
It does vary. Sometimes one feels discovered, and another time one wants to understand it better.

Second Questioner:
I've become interested in common sense, which for me has not been a subject that I have paid much attention to. It appears to me that I seem to abandon my common sense when I'm close to a different state in myself.

Dr. Welch:
What is common sense? Common to all the senses, yes? It looks right, smells right, listens right, tastes right, touches right—you know? It always appealed to me that Gurdjieff's worldview could really be called brilliant common sense. His psychology is so simple. It's not full of elaborate embroidery. There's no patois. There's no jargon. There's no special gobbledy-gook around it. He's not afraid to say, "Bring reason to it. Think."

Am I in touch with something that is properly referred to as common sense? Common sense suggests that there is an equilibrium in all of us, something that can come to a place that is both pragmatically and theoretically in our best interest—not from the point of view of smoothing our feathers, but which corresponds to our best intelligence and our best data.

Same Person:
It's as if I lose a certain basic grounding because I'm hoping to experience something grander than my ordinary state. So, when there is a taste of presence, there actually seems to be a certain confusion in me.

Dr. Welch:
Are you dreaming? Could that be?

Same Person:
It certainly could be. Why do say that?

Dr. Welch:
Well, because you said that, with the appearance in you of what you feel to be presence, you became confused. Is that true? Did I hear that properly?

Same Person:
Yes. My impression is that there is something genuine taking place, and that I'm lost in an assessment of it.

Dr. Welch:
What do you mean by an assessment?

Same Person:
Well, I suppose that I mean that even while it's there in *me*, I'm not there in *it*.

Dr. Welch:
What stands in your way then?

Same Person:
Well, I could say it's *me*, but...

Dr. Welch:
Wait. Wait. Simpler than that, maybe. Because of course that's true. But isn't there something here that relates to a wandering attention—a commenting, a movement into assessment? This interferes with the experience, and then perhaps the experience is over. And this movement into assessment isn't something that our common sense is applying itself to at all.

It's not an easy circumstance to find oneself in. But do you have an idea of how it ought to be? Surely not.

Same Person:
It seems to me that I've lost the simple, ordinary "me" in this experience—the one who is speaking now. Where do I go when there is a sense of presence in myself?

Dr. Welch:
All my "me"s are ordinary. And they're not bad. And they haven't left. They may be silent for a while, but they'll turn up again. And they're not in charge, in any event. Indeed, when one experiences this, a lot of these wandering attentions are dropped.

As the moment of the experience disappears, I go off in associations again. They may be very solid, good commonsensical associations, but they have nothing to do with the experience. They're comments, judgments, or, as you put it, assessments, and they may even make sense. But they certainly are busy making notes, aren't they? Have I misunderstood?

Same Person:
No.

Dr. Welch:
I think that moments of illumination, moments of wholeness, moments of sudden clarity, are moments. They're not permanent states.

Same Person:
I have the impression that I thought what I felt, and I felt what I thought. That's not an experience I've had with that kind of clarity before.

Dr. Welch:
And what happened to your thought when you felt what you thought?

You don't have to answer that.

You know, the work is all about the relation of the centers. The appearance of true feeling in the presence of thought is something very moving. I'm not so sure about thinking what I feel. I'm sure that what happens, for me, more often than not, is that the critic appears. But there is something about the awakening of a real feeling, in a moment of thought that did not have this, that is so enlivening, extending, illuminating: making larger connections. It's another perception of things.

. . . .

You know, I was touched for a moment by the almost miraculous sense in which, under certain circumstances, one really is in the presence of a stranger in oneself. This is not the stranger that is a threat, but a curious recognition of what it is not to know, and further, not to believe that one really does know somewhere. One can actually see that one doesn't know. This is an unknown area, and it somehow takes the shape and the form of the one who recognizes this. This is certainly not a common experience, but when it takes place, it seems, somehow, so true. This is the appropriate place in which to be in touch with what we call the unknown.

One doesn't really know oneself, but one can see the reality of this. It is a warmly startling thing to meet this. It is not something that is a confrontation, or strange, but just, "Oh!" The recognition doesn't have any detail of what the stranger is, but only that, "Yes, I don't know this." There is only the sense of not knowing, and that this is the place to look. And then it doesn't last very long.

Third Questioner:

I have always assumed that there should be an answer to the question "Who am I?" but recently it occurred to me—and I was surprised when it did—that possibly there isn't an answer. And maybe there isn't supposed to be an answer. Maybe one is supposed to keep asking the question without ever expecting an answer.

Dr. Welch:

Certainly, the exploration doesn't end. One doesn't expect an answer that just closes the door. The mystery of life is not so simple. Even in ordinary terms, the mystery of life, in the terms of the Bible, "passeth all understanding."

Self-knowledge is a spiritual path where one doesn't anticipate sprouting wings or taking off, but rather being more enriched by the depth of the mystery. And it's an extraordinary thing that I don't give any attention, in all my days and in all the hours of my days, to the miracle of the fact that I'm alive. It's not so easy to entertain that miracle.

On the other hand, it's the one thing that is the *sine qua non* of the whole enterprise. Any interference with this being alive is the only radical thing that can happen. Everything else is not at the root.

But my perception of these realities is very elusive. And if anybody thinks they have an answer, it's just fantasy.

. . . .

I don't know any experts at waking up. I know a great many people who have been undertaking to make the veil less opaque. But one should not confuse the aspiration with becoming. This work does not guarantee that one is going to be "Mr. Conscious." That isn't the point. One finds out for oneself that this awareness, this consciousness, is not something that lasts very long, nor something that is readily seized, nor is it usable as something.

But there are degrees. There are levels. There are possibilities of being less in a dream, less in a state of relative unawareness. I don't know anything that Gurdjieff ever promised except that one wouldn't sleep quite so comfortably after undertaking to pursue his point of view. There's no promise of serenity, or superman, or superwoman—all these fantasies. It's a continued exploration.

Sometimes one is touched by the rare person who appears to be in touch with an inner reality, and when they are confronted by something, they bring quite a different point of view. One has the sense that they're in another place in themselves that is curiously awakening. But such encounters are not so frequent.

We're all attracted by the sniff of accomplishing something. The whole West is like this. We can't get away from it.

Fourth Questioner:
It feels very much that I do want to accomplish something. When I came here, I was straining to have a question. And then I realized that I haven't seen you in so many years, and it was very emotional. I could feel myself relax, and I felt that it's okay just to be here with you. So, the question I have from that is, "Why do I strain? Why do I wish to accomplish?"

Dr. Welch:
I think the Western notion is of a linear pursuit of an aim, over barriers, to a conclusion that is the result of struggle and endurance. This produces a lot of strain in us, a lot of tension. We have this mode of pursuit, so we tend to bring to our efforts what we bring to everything else in our life.

But one's experience very often turns out to be moments of clarity that are electronic in character, not linear. How often have you heard someone say, "It seemed to have no relation to this thing that I call my effort; it was a gift"? It was something that came under conditions that were quite remarkable, and the conditions seemed to have brought it.

At the same time, that kind of thing doesn't seem to occur for those who don't try it. So, it's not so easy to say that all you have to do is just lie back. There is something about the best effort we can make that moves us toward inner order, toward inner quiet, toward inner silence, toward inner sensory experience, toward a relation to the attention. Remember, man is an extraordinary organism, almost infinitely variable and complicated, with all kinds of backups, wondrous maneuvers, cellular capacitance: an amazing feeling, and thinking, and mobile vehicle.

And we're just a little pie cut of the potentiality of this organism. We have something that can focus and that can, from time to time, show quite a capacity to be rigorous. We can approach the idea of objectivity towards ourselves and see how terribly difficult this is. We can see how remote we are from being true Solomons about ourselves. And yet one hears the call. It keeps calling; it keeps saying, "Look. Try."

What does Gurdjieff say about self-observation? He says, "You can't do it, but you must try." When you try you will uncover what you need to know. But don't imagine that this is some sort of version of putting yourself under a microscope and taking a look. It's not so easy. Gurdjieff takes the trouble to say, "You will discover that it's not something that you can do." That doesn't mean that it is something impossible for man, but something that is far more elusive to us, as we are, than it was at first glance, when we thought, "Well, the thing to do is observe yourself." And most people in the Work talk about self-observation as though they knew all about it.

Fifth Questioner:
It's disconcerting to see how my attitudes are in everything. I do feel some hope there, because just seeing it has already loosened its hold. Part of the experience is almost like becoming more childlike, but there is a certain anxiety about that as well. Although I have moments of experiencing a freedom, I'm mostly still in the clutch of my reactions, and I see that those reactions are unbecoming. I do recognize what you say about not trying to

reform myself. But there's a certain road I have to travel to be able to have the courage to look at that, to bear my manifestations. I realize that I need to see myself more, but I have an anxiety about that.

Dr. Welch:
Most people are not flattered by what they see, you know. But the idea of attitude is interesting from many points of view. Ouspensky used to say, "The one thing you can change is your attitude." He didn't say you could change it forever. But if you find that you know what your attitude is, it is possible, in our present state, to confront that attitude, and to see it, and to try on another one. Instead of being the report card-writing monitor of all my little sins and all the obvious sins of others—all the things that I accumulate by such observations—it's possible to play a kind of role. I can drop some of these unperceived convictions until I see that they are part of my way of looking at things, what I bring to a situation—a way that is far from being open. And I just try to say, "Look, all bets are off." Everybody that I know all about I don't really know at all, if I think about it. So, I will try now to have an attitude that is a listening, and a looking, and a responding, without having always to come to a conclusion about the person I'm talking with. Yes?

Same Person:
I feel hopeful that you say that that's possible.

Dr. Welch:
Well, I'm not an authority on these things, but I always was touched by the fact that Ouspensky said this quite firmly. You know, the Dalai Llama was asked by a newspaperman whether he was really just an ordinary fellow, like everybody else. And he said, "Yes, except that every morning, when I get up, I adjust my attitude." I thought that was rather interesting.

But, you know, we're all victims of our attitudes. It's very difficult to be in familiar circumstances without having the attitude that you know what you're going to meet. Or your attitude may be: "I have no idea what's going on here, but they're probably a bunch of idiots anyway." There are all kind of variants on this theme.

The interesting thing is not so much to be a designer of a perfect attitude, but rather to determine whether one indeed has attitudes or not. One doesn't see them as something artificially imposed. I don't see that that's my view: "That's how I see it, and that's how things must be, because that's what I see." It's a curious kind of circular thing. But I don't think of myself as having an attitude; I think of myself as damn well knowing what I'm doing and seeing—not questioning at all.

It's something to explore. There isn't any "how to" here. The whole enterprise is exploration, usually in the face of somebody who knows all about it already. We don't quite say that, but, you know...

There was an old friend of ours, who's been dead now for some time, who used to say, "You know, we think the work is theory and we're real. But it's really just the other way around."

You know, this is a great array here—all these people. Love is something that isn't widely understood. Love is seeing. And I think everybody in this room has a wish to be here, not to be absent. I don't mean whether you come or don't come, but when you're here, not to be absent. Something awakens in this room, for me anyway. It's very alive, and it's so interesting that you never hear the cracked bell in this room. Nobody lies. You know, the cracked pot sound that isn't a nice "tung," but "bock."

Pondering. Degree of failure. Intervening in one's life.
A sense of hopefulness. Change in the habitual terrain.

First Questioner:
I'm interested in the question of pondering. Instead of sitting, sometimes, I've started trying to weigh what's going on in my life, and it seems to me, at least intellectually, that if I could realize what I know, or understand what we all talked about and studied, then it would be much more substantial, and then I would be much more able to be. But I'm unable to do that.

Dr. Welch:
For example, what sort of thing would you undertake to ponder?

Same Person:
Well, for example, the direction of my relationship with someone who is close to me, or specific problems that disturb me with them.

Dr. Welch:
Have you undertaken to ponder things that you assume that you really know something about? Would you undertake, for example, to ponder the question of self-observation? Is man asleep? Am I? What is our work? Does this kind of thing present itself to you as being a subject for undertaking whatever it is we mean by weighing something? By pondering? Is that what you're speaking of?

Same Person:
Yes, that's the kind of direction that I think, perhaps, I need, because, sometimes, although I feel close, I get lost in the practical details, or I get taken.

Dr. Welch:
Or one realizes that one doesn't really know the practical details? Perhaps? Go on.

Same Person:
So, my question is how can I help myself get into the state where I'm able to begin to really digest what's happening to me. Does it naturally arise out of self-observation—if I could do such a thing—or is it also a question of finding the time and the place, and the right attitude, the right relaxation, the right...?

Dr. Welch:
What do you mean by "the right"?

Same Person:
One that allows me not to be taken.

Dr. Welch:
Is it an option not to be taken? Maybe this is just exactly something one can see.

You can't sweep the whole place and get a nice clean sidewalk with no leaves on it. There isn't any "how to" here. I can make the effort to be in touch with the possibility of another scale, of another place in myself that is available—not to my little box of worms, but to my role as a member of the human condition. There is the possibility of a relation to the scale of mankind, a relation to organic life. What does that really mean? Where am I now? What is different about what I would propose to not lose, when my ordinary, everyday attitude enters—which I can examine, because today is every day? Where was I before the idea occurred to me?

And I see that there are lots of little tensions that I hadn't been aware of, and I realize that much of my life is concerned with the impact of my bodily tensions. I think, perhaps, in order to come to some place in myself that could give me the possibility of something that is in the direction of what I understand to be pondering, it would be helpful at this point, perhaps, to get in touch with myself. And I find that my relation to myself can be enhanced, in a way, if these tensions, which I'm quite unintentionally in touch with at the moment, lead to an effort to be in touch with the sensory nature of my extremities and my body. And it occurs to me that I've often been told that there is a relation between the various aspects of myself that I represent, in one way or another, as the head, and the heart, and the body.

Gurdjieff has often said that the one "rent in the tent" is the relative availability of the body as something that can be experienced—certainly when one is undertaking a start—far more readily than I can undertake to be in touch with my thought or my feelings. I know from experience that my thoughts will upset whatever I'm doing and will take me away, as he puts it, "discovering America." And that I'm lost in my feelings and in my emotions much more than I can pretend to be able to observe them. If they exist, they usually have me.

But there's a possibility of coming in somewhere near to the head and the body. And I may not be able to begin at a very high place in myself, but I can begin, wherever I am, to have a relatively conscious experience of myself. If I'm going to ponder, I can't just wiseacre with my head, nor can I get sentimental about my feelings. I have to begin somewhere so that maybe I can go in the direction of work, which, among other things, has to do with the relationship of the centers to one another. I would wish to find myself more nearly in touch with a sense of how small my circumstances are, and how immeasurable is the role of mankind, and the actual nothingness of me at the same time that I'm the center of the universe. How can that be?

And so, to the extent that I can collect something in myself, and if my attention doesn't, too abruptly and too often, escape my relation to it, it's possible for something to appear that is another way of thinking that doesn't allow me to slip away and dream, but to begin to ponder.

Is what I'm doing something about self-observation? I rather suspect that it's an aspect of it. Does this touch you as a possible beginning? Is there somebody in me who, though not unified, is less scattered? Is there somebody who's going to try to undertake to be present to what, at its highest possible level for me, might be called "being-reason," something that, again, I don't understand, but is an idea that appeals to me?

Does this correspond to what you've looked for?

Same Person:
Yes.

Dr. Welch:
And what question has it raised?

Same Person:
I found that when I tried sensation like that, very often feeling would appear, and then I would get taken by a pleasant nostalgia of some sort, or a feeling about someone that I was close to, a feeling very close to sentimentality. Then it was difficult for me to come back.

Dr. Welch:
This is certainly futile, if one comes to some kind of wandering emotional sentimentality about oneself, but perhaps you could find that something awakens in you that is related to a feeling-perception of the real scale of what you are undertaking. And this suddenly associates with the idea that Gurdjieff has spoken of so much: feeling what you think and thinking what you feel. Maybe, when the body is related as well, one can, as he put it, begin to think like a man rather than like a dog. Because this awakens the possibility of a relationship among the three aspects of our being that we share: reason, feeling, and sensory participation in one's presence. The absence of that relationship is what characterizes my usual scatteredness. And my scatteredness now is less pervasive.

And I don't expect that I'm going to have a lot of illuminating thoughts, but I can stay with this relative availability. I can be relatively more available, relatively less identified with my crummy little ambitions, not whole, but less partial, and without expectations that are beyond my possibility at my present level. The sensory nature of my body is still with me. It is far more relaxed than when we started. The little points of tension are not missed. I've heard that maybe something can be awakened in me when my head and my body are more nearly related one to the other. But I don't want to imagine about that. I have no necessity—no right, in a way—to expect something that is a result. It is much more a waiting to see, a waiting...to see. Because it isn't my little ego that's going to do this, although it's not something that I'm very successful at evading. It's going to take its place somewhere else, because I'm all alone now, and I don't anticipate for a moment making any concessions to that. I wish to let it find its own place.

Maybe I'm on the road to something like pondering, and if I'm not, I'll find out. If I can stay with this, I may not put something on the scale and weigh it, but I may at least come to someplace in myself where the difficulty becomes less baffling and more nearly a place of quiet, inner perception—not of something that I will call understanding, but of something that may be nearer to a place in which something is possible in me that's not sleep and dreams. And I don't want get stuck on words. I don't think I could say that I know what pondering is, but it's not the usual associative pursuit of a superficial understanding of something.

Maybe we can try this ourselves. Maybe others are interested in undertaking something of this kind. But it's something that is an exploration, not a series of steps.

What do I want? What do I wish? What do I need? What stands in my way?

Second Questioner:
I'd like to speak about an experience that happened this summer. We worked very hard this summer. In Toronto we had two intensive work periods. We had numerous weekends at the farm. There was a lot of responsibility, which we approached with our best effort. We had a planning meeting that went on quite late. We

began with a sitting, and we ended with a sitting. And I undertook to work during the meeting with a simple task: to remember
my body sitting on the chair. At the end of the meeting, during
the sitting, I realized I'd forgotten, and I hadn't worked, and I was
struck with a feeling-perception of the enormity of what we are
trying to do. I was very moved, and at the same time, I didn't feel
that it was hopeless, just that it was enormously difficult, that in
the face of all our work together and all the support, that there
are enormous forces keeping me asleep. I began to wonder if I
have the energy for this work. All that I'm given, by my teachers,
and by Mr. Gurdjieff, and through the Movements, and through
our work together... And I am unable to *be here now*.

Dr. Welch:
Who sees that?

Same Person:
I don't know...

Dr. Welch:
Yes, you do.

Same Person:
...but maybe the one that weeps.

Dr. Welch:
If one sees one's inability, one's incapacity, one's vulnerability,
this begins to touch on something that is perhaps our level of
self-observation. What would you like to see? Something other? A
muscular angel? You know?

When one speaks about all those forces that are against us,
we're very tempted to become another one of the numerous victims of the world. Everybody's a victim of something. It's said
that we have got enough energy somewhere, if we don't waste
it *too* excessively. And perhaps one arrives at a place, if one really wishes something other than what one has, to begin to see in

oneself where one's energy goes. One begins to find places where it slips away, perhaps. Or one begins to become interested in the idea of tension, interested in the idea of preoccupation, interested in the idea of considering, interested in the idea of memory, interested in recollecting moments that were other than these moments of dispersion.

And instead of discovering that one, as they say, can't do it, one becomes more interested in what one does do, in what one does allow. And who is telling me that my level of effort is so incapacitating and so absent in force that I have labeled myself with a question of "Maybe I shouldn't be here and trying this?" But this is ignoring my terrain, my personal terrain. There's plenty of information around about what one can undertake, and then one can see why one fails, where one fails. One can even fall in love with saying that the degree of failure today was less than the degree of failure yesterday. I mean it's not unreasonable at all. That's where we are; that's why we should not imagine we're somewhere else.

Same Person:
I don't think I value enough the one that sees. I've been told that I want to see what's not there, and I believe it now. I'm beginning to see that that's true. I want to be here now, and I want to be completely occupied and not preoccupied.

Dr. Welch:
Why are you here? I'm not asking you to answer that question. I don't it mean that way. But there's a motive somewhere, deep within you, of why you're here. It isn't just a bad habit. You know, it was Mme de Salzmann, I think, who said that when people come together, if no one remembers *why*, there is no sense in their coming together. Something is possible only if one really undertakes to remember *why* I am here.

What is another question. But nonetheless, one can ponder this: "Why am I here?" And be ruthless with oneself. Maybe I didn't want to be seen as absent. There are all kinds of things that can happen. But nevertheless, one can examine, and one can remember that there is hope, way deep down. This is not a trivial or frivolous undertaking. To the extent that one can, one can weigh the seriousness of one's search. And I don't mean the solemnity. But we fluctuate; we go up and down. We see that we don't always so much see what's taking place as become lost in it. And then afterwards we talk about what we saw. Did we see? Or were we lost?

Same Person:
I feel that this is very important, this capacity to see what is really there, to see it, and to allow it to be there. Many times, that's where I get distracted—by a judgment.

Dr. Welch:
Yes, if I've begun to chat about how terrible it is to myself, something is lost.

Same Person:
And my refrain, which is, "I'm wasting time."

Dr. Welch:
Yes.
     And that, again, is in retrospect, isn't it; it isn't recognized at the moment.

Same Person:
I can see tricks that I try to play. Maybe some of them aren't so stupid. I try to relax. I try to let go of tensions. Then I try to find something that's not there.

Dr. Welch:
Well, to see that there's nothing there is also difficult, but not without its clarity. To see nothing is to know something about that moment. And can I stay there? What does it mean, *nothing*? Do I see that I see nothing? This is another impression of myself that I already have made a judgment about, rather than stayed with. Am I there? Now? What do I expect?

I have to come back to why I am here. And I come back, to remember what? Why I am here. And if I find nothing, this is a very good place to begin. At least I'm not filled with illusion. I don't find imagination and dreams. Maybe I can undertake to be silent here, instead of running a conversation about it that confirms my theory of personal doom.

Third Questioner:
I recently had a number of impressions in a relatively short time that were so different that they widened the scale of the question for me. It began as I walked from the train to my car where I undertook to try to see myself for the duration of the walk, and more or less did not. It came and went, but more or less went. But there were moments of an impression of a center of gravity. In a sense, an impression of some "seer" inside, that actually, for a moment, was there to see. And it had a very clear taste.

Today, at some point over the course of the day, I found myself—I noticed it somewhat after the fact—reacting negatively to something that happened with my wife. And rationally, I saw flaws in my reaction: that I was reacting very much from the perspective of an ego's hurt feelings. But what was taking place in me wasn't just the reaction. It was actually a tug-of-war of some kind. I wasn't going with the reaction. I wasn't not going with it, either. In a way, it was all percolating under the surface. There was some part of me that wasn't totally willing to give itself up to the reaction.

Then toward the evening today, there was a period in which I tried to see into myself and felt very much lost in moments or movements of inner considering. Again, it was only a fleeting impression, but there was this sense of looking in and seeing nothing but a sense of disorder. There was no longer a sense of some perceiver in the midst of it.

And then in the sitting, there was another impression, which was again very different, but seemed important to the overall picture. And that was essentially me as a relatively honest, simple person trying to understand, trying to be there in an ordinary sense, bringing my best effort to it, without a capital "E." And my attention was with a lower case "a." But there was a certain sincerity about me there that seems important. It was as if there were a basic marshaling of thought and feeling to that endeavor that itself invited an impression of the whole being greater than the sum of its parts.

There came a "look from above," and I didn't bring it, and I don't know how it happened. But it seemed to relate to the fact that there was basically someone there trying to understand this in an honest, direct way, not trying to figure out a gimmick or an answer, but looking at this more from the point of view that this is a big question, that it's not going to be answered overnight, and there's a lifetime of serious study necessary. Somehow that ordinary approach seemed very important for that moment.

So, these experiences, falling so close to one another, show such a variety of experiences and impressions of myself that I can't draw any kind of conclusion, but it certainly showed that there is a lot to be seen.

Dr. Welch:
But this is what you saw. Of course, you didn't draw a conclusion. You saw that you were many. I think what you described at the end is very touching. This is an aspect of availability. I'm not sure to what I wish to be available, but I wish not to be closed. You brought your common sense. You brought your unadorned best side, the one who came to listen. There was the one who felt the suction into this old familiar role of being outraged and conflicted, but at the same time, there was somebody who said, "No, I don't have to do that again." You saw something that was an old repetition, and you didn't really believe in it with the conviction that one often has when one's self-righteousness and all the rest of it come to the fore. So, you were influenced by a sidelong glance, maybe not a full observation, but something that you saw was not as "sleeping-a-taking" as it often is. Am I wrong? Is that what you said?

Same Person:
Yes.

Dr. Welch:

It's what I heard, and I was very touched by it, because one knows that one can be in the midst of a classical repetition of a reaction, particularly in the circumstances of a marriage. There you are with your wife, and you have this reaction. It's an old story; it's something that you know well. But to stop in the middle of that, not as the hero, but just: "I don't have to go on with this despite of the pull of it." The pull of it looks so fragile in a way, so kind of fixed. You don't have to go with it.

And there's a moment of freedom, and one sees that something changes. And one is not, at that moment, the slave of one's inner compulsion. It is a very hopeful kind of variant of there being, maybe not a real guardian at the door, but maybe something like a security guard. There's a nice kind of quite spontaneous emergence of, not a customary slave, but the slave who suddenly says, "Maybe...maybe." And then it doesn't persist, but at the same time, something changed. And this is not something you planned, not something you decided to do. But it was, jolly well, the result of a lot of other things you tried to do, because if you never try anything, nothing takes place.

When something does take place, one cannot say that it is because of this or that. But in the absence of "this" and "that," nothing happens. One can do all kinds of wrong things, and try, and have all kinds of strains and stresses, but a linear pursuit over a lot of barriers is not the work. At the same time, a linear pursuit over a lot of barriers does something about the instrument. It makes it more available for something intentional. It makes it more available for the unanticipated look that sees, because one has been putting oneself into a place that is different than just floating. Maybe it's just trying to stay even. This has its uncharted effect. So, one knows very well that one can't claw one's way. But in the absence of a certain amount of clawing, the instrument isn't very available. So, it's a paradox.

The whole idea is to bring something intentional, either by decision or because it appears, into what is otherwise a whole mélange of reflexes. These reflexes have been cultivated without a real eye to anything except getting on with things, of finding patterns of behavior that, more or less, get a little hamburger into the refrigerator without interrupting your range of mechanical activities. One is intervening in that life from time to time and finding that it's going on. This is really what you were saying: you were intervening in your life and you saw what was going on. And it was *going on*. It wasn't what you intended, but you brought some intention to it. You saw the impact of somebody attending to your life, and it was not a supervisor, but an observer.

Fourth Questioner:
I see now how I've often taken work on myself in the wrong way and turned it into a technique, or something that is actually self-calming. This is something I do all the time, with everything. Self-observation has to be dynamic, and in the moment, and related to the way I am. The words don't do justice to what I just understood, but instead of real observation, I imagine that I'm going to find some state, and then, from there, I'm going to observe what enters, and in that way maintain the state. Do you see what I mean?

Dr. Welch:
Yes, I do.

Same Person:
And so, it never works because I'm fighting myself all the time. I suppose it's valid enough to try. That's all I have sometimes.

Dr. Welch:
Well, you know, in the absence of undertaking certain things, one never has the occasion for observing oneself doing it all cockeyed. We're not very good at this. We make, as Gurdjieff says, "cacophonous noises" when we do this, and people hate us. That wonderful word "self-calming." God knows we turn to this a great deal. All of

us. We wish to be reassured and sent into a nice state of knowing something, and then we see how thin that is. But it seems to me that the kinds of experiences we've been talking about tonight are really where the fabric, the networking, of our lives is taking place. And it's *there* that we see these private capacities and incapacities of ourselves. It's there that we have the possibility of being far more in touch with how we are than how we almost always *think* we are.

Remember that thing of Gurdjieff's that begins: "You are not who you think you are"? Is what I think I am such a potent hypnotist that I go right on believing that I am what I know very well somewhere I'm not? He goes on to say all kinds of things that are very hard to swallow. And very wrong to swallow unless one can verify. But I think it's interesting that what we see is not a final critique of how we are, but rather more information about how, in fact, we can see without making a final judgment. That isn't the end of anything. As we were saying, we are one thing one moment and quite another thing at another moment.

There's something about a certain kind of ebullience that's in the direction of this thing that we all think of as joy. When, for a moment, there is a suspension of fear, a sense of affirmation appears at a place where one is no longer immersed in oneself. It may not last very long, but there's a great sense of hopefulness that can emerge. One can be at a place of the sourest kind of self-abnegation, and considering, and so on. Then a note is struck that changes the scale. And suddenly one is touched by quite another spectrum of life, and one sees that one's preoccupation is a big lie—just the old, sore, embodiment of fear and reaction and imagination and all the usual junk. But then one is lifted to another place. And one feels a sort of relief at being able to turn to a large, unanswerable question, even though one doesn't necessarily describe it that way. There's someone there who is undertaking to bring some approximation of "being-reason" to this. And then one is in touch with another level of being—not the level of an angel, but more nearly the level of a "man without quotation marks," more nearly in that direction.

Fifth Questioner:
I was in India recently. And because of the very different surroundings, I couldn't be my usual self, in a way. The surroundings
didn't behave the way my surroundings usually do. And I just had
a moment where I felt that I wasn't who I think I am. I felt that
most of the time I am not that person that I think I am. I can't even
really put it into words, but it was very frightening. I suddenly
experienced the person who I think I am as not having any substance...you know, just the conversation in my mind. Do you know
what I'm saying?

Dr. Welch:
Yes. Yes, I do.

Same Person:
I felt that I couldn't stay with it at all, because it was so frightening. But it was like suddenly seeing that most of the time you're
just not there: that there's this story, and the story is all there is.

Dr. Welch:
Pretty hard business you've got there. But it's true. And as you
found, it's not easy to stay with that.

Same Person:
Well, maybe I shouldn't have even brought it up and talked about
it.

Dr. Welch:
No, it's good that you brought it.
    I think that there's something about travel, where one's im-
pressions are all so unaccustomed. It evokes a different response
because it doesn't correspond to the chorus of responses that one
has a picture of, an image of. I think it's very interesting that what
you saw was that the exchange didn't have any of the familiar re-
assurances in it. Am I right?

Same Person:

Yes. It happened after a few weeks of sort of being shocked by the unaccustomed surroundings. It was as if I briefly saw this, experienced this, out of the corner of my eye. And then I couldn't bear it.

Dr. Welch:

It's quite something to be struck by a habitual mechanism that goes on in my life. I think this is not easily weighed, not easily understood. But it gives one a clue to the imagination that goes on in what I think I am.

Same Person:

I was walking, and my usual story was going on: "I feel like this, and I'm tired of this, and I'm like this, and then I'm going to do this, and I'm like that..." and suddenly, I just experienced myself in another way, as though there was a gap between the person who was there and the story.

Dr. Welch:

It shows how much I am a reactor to perceived impulses that emerge from the circumstances in which I live. In unusual circumstances we are much more alert to the manifestations of very simple ordinary things that we are so familiar with that we don't see our responses at all. But there's something that awakens consciousness, that shocks us awake, in these circumstances, because we see something that has given a new interest to this extraordinary life—otherwise known as "ordinary life." There I am, in a situation where all the landmarks are changed, and all the impressions that arise from people are not necessarily beyond imagination or beyond perceiving, but they're all different. There's a whole new ambiance there that awakens something in me, because I am not able to correspond to it in my usual way. The fingers have changed a little, and suddenly my music is cacophonous to me. I don't respond with something that corresponds.

It raises the question of just how responsible I am for what I think I know about myself, and how clear is my perception of this. If I have to come to a conclusion, I have to say there's a lot that I just don't know. When my mask is torn off by circumstances—and I'm pretty sure that there's not very much behind that mask—I go to great lengths to keep my mask up. It is difficult to be sure of what is behind my mask, and I don't acknowledge it as a mask, really.

One cannot overestimate the impact of suddenly changing the whole terrain of people and places and things and activities and emotions, and so on. It's very different from First Avenue, New York, where I just don't have any problem about who I am. But the question, which has been raised in India, may have some validity in New York.

But again, it's to be seen, not to be lamented.

I want to tip my hat and say thank you to these honest people, speaking from their interiors and awakening, for all of us, another look at how we are. A lot of self-observation. It doesn't begin to cover the terrain, but nonetheless it has its possibility, its potential.

[A long period of silence]

First Questioner:

I've been trying to work, in small ways, with the notion that our ordinary life is actually extraordinary. In my life, when I remember, I've been trying to get a sense of all the various functionings and what's going on. There's always a great variety of external functioning, for sure, and internal functioning too: how I see, how I hear, sensations of all sorts. And sometimes there's a glimmer of what you say, that it is extraordinary. It seems to me I need to take this effort into the domain of the psyche as well. This doesn't really go anywhere if I don't get deeper, to the core of myself. With inner considering, for example, it's almost impossible to observe it, not to be caught up with it.

With any of a range of psychological things, I kind of know them in my own way, which means I don't really know them at all. I don't see them from the perspective of functioning, or, I suppose, from the perspective of what is. And it seems to me that there are a great many ways in which I can fool myself, and that even in the initial effort it's awfully easy to think I'm seeing something when I'm not.

Dr. Welch:

Yes. You're speaking of the difference between being lost in something and then later saying that this is what I saw, rather than what I was lost in. Is that what I hear you saying?

Same Person:

Yes, with psychological manifestations, I tend to be lost in them at the time. Often there's a kind of discomfort that takes me, and then I can't look at it at all, because I'm wrapped up in the discomfort. It occurs in a very familiar way, but it's not seeing it. On the other hand, I've had the rare experience of actually also being alive, in some mysterious way, to see this take place, and it relates to a kind of functioning. Considering relates to a kind of functioning. You have to have considerations about what you do next. We're in motion, doing things.

Dr. Welch:
The difficulty is to separate, to some extent, from the content and to undertake to be more nearly aware of what one can think of as the mill that is doing the grist, because the mechanism is always the same. And the material is always, or almost always, very seductive. Do you agree with that?

Same Person:
Yes.

Dr. Welch:
And the only possible detachment from this is in the direction of what we've heard called, over and over, "a look from above." One has a recurrent sour taste of this kind of experience and it always occurs by a mechanism that I'm unaware of, because I take it as my own. It's very difficult to bring myself to the place where I'm sufficiently unseduced by the contents, where I can begin to entertain the idea that my behavior, my manifestation, my inner life, is an example of the level of my being, not of my singular character. It's the one place where there is more common experience, where I can recognize my strange preoccupation with a mask, with an impression that I wish to make, with what I fear being exposed, with my notion of outer darkness—all these things that have a largely imaginary fabric.

What is more interesting is the effort to try and be present, to be aware of, to be alive to, the mechanism, rather than the contents, and to begin to see something about my small repertoire of these tawdry defenses of the mask. It's very hard not to be contemptuous of oneself for this, because one fails to see that this is how one is, at this level of being—where we are. It's one of the aspects of self-observation that is clearly difficult.

Same Person:
I think I have a kind of mental confusion that sometimes may even hinder me, which is thinking that I have to be quicker to catch what's going on inside. It may even be true, but when I take it as a mental notion, it doesn't help.

Dr. Welch:
At its onset, you mean.

Same Person:
At its onset. What happens is very fast. Maybe it's not contradictory, but it seems you are saying that "seeing it from above" leads to a different type of an effort, in a sense. As you say, there's no method, but I can get stuck in a way of thinking about it that doesn't help.

Dr. Welch:
It's true. There isn't any "how to" about it. The suffering that preoccupies one is not something that is brought about by volition. This is the suffering that is not intentional. It's wasteful; it can exhaust me. And there is no sense in kicking it under the rug, or trying to get rid of it, but rather one needs to move toward it, to become closer to it, to see where it, in fact, leads. What is this combination of self-distress, and fear, and all the absurdity that is involved with these really rather shabby experiences? One can try and bring oneself to it: to say, "All right. What is it that has me here?" Not what is the content of it, but what is the nature of this? Where do I think it leads? One can bring something active to it, not active in the sense of participating in it, but undertaking to be present to it, to see it, because, naturally, one wishes to escape from it.

The effort is not to reform, but, in a modest way, to transform, in that there can be another level of examination of this machinery.

One can begin to undertake to see it for what it is. And the more intense the experience, the more difficulty one has in undertaking this. But this is a place of struggle. In a sense, the struggle is to accept it for what it is, not for what it seems to be to my psyche.

Second Questioner:

I had an encounter today with being occupied. I had three morning meetings, and all of them had left me with what I saw as difficulties for myself. So something instinctively told me that I should walk home. Something was moving, and I had this feeling that if my body could at least take the movement, then maybe it could come out of my head. Because everything in my head was going round and round, trying to solve these problems. After about twenty blocks I realized quite clearly that, in ordinary terms, this effort wasn't getting me anywhere. I was just going over and over this stuff. The situation was such that I wasn't going to be able to solve them, even if I could, until later in the day. So I could really try something else. So I did try, as we have tried before, to sense my feet on the ground and keep out of my head.

And what interested me was why it was so interesting to be up there where it was a problem and not something nice. And why it was not of real interest to try this. But I kept trying and I saw, in a way, that I didn't wish to be present to now. That was the difficulty. I really didn't want to be here now. Part of me wanted to be ahead and get this problem solved, and then everything would be all right. But then I started to feel, "Well, this is life; it isn't really a problem; it's not actually going to go away. It's life; it's ongoing." And so, while I couldn't get out of my head completely, my thinking about my difficulties with this became somewhat broader. I was still, in a way, defending myself, but I began to see that the problem was that I was, again, needing to reaffirm myself. I was grateful for the Work, because it made a difference.

Dr. Welch:

You made an effort to intervene and do something appropriate with a lot of stirred up energy, which is to walk. Twenty blocks is a reasonable chore. Then it shifted, if I heard you correctly, and you began to weigh this thing. Am I right?

Same Person:
Yes.

Dr. Welch:
And this again was an intervention from a reasonable place. After all, we don't have God's spyglass. We have to use what we have. And you entered into this with reason. Someday this may be "being-reason." It was your best substitute for "being-reason." And something clarified. Am I wrong?

Same Person:
Well, I didn't just start to reason, but it was something about trying to get out of the head and into the body that seemed to allow different kinds of thoughts to come.

Dr. Welch:
Well, yes, but one can't be a chooser about this. The effort was an intervention, and it was by way of the head. What form it took, what way, I don't know. It's not so easy to be sure about those neurotransmitters up there; they do a lot of things. But in any event, it was more nearly a change of tempo, a change of emphasis; something moved.

It strikes me that, without applying some formula, you, in fact, came to yourself and were less pushed and more nearly aware of the nature of this. As you put it, "This is a good life. This is not something I'm going to turn a key and fix."

These are certainly efforts at being present to yourself. And they don't carry large metaphysical signs that one is transformed. It's not that, but it is the difference between passivity and an effort at some sort of action, rather than reaction. It is very different from just suffering, from just feeling wronged, or feeling under a threat, or feeling under some demand that one is going to have great difficulty dealing with. No, it appeared in you that it was an aspect of your journey; it was a place in your life. And it took on something other than the characteristic of what one is when life is unattended. It was an effort to attend to your life.

And one doesn't have a great deal of expertise about this, nor are there necessarily words that say it very well for us. But the inner movement was, I should say, in the direction of awareness and less identification—coming nearer to the place where there is that almost impossible thing called objectivity.

. . . .

Third Questioner:
Under certain circumstances, like these, I'm noticing that there is a part that I can play to reawaken, in a way. And it is almost as if it's all there, but I'm just not there to see that it's all there. There's a part that is not as grandiose as I might imagine it to be, but it's quite definite. I begin to sense that this is what I miss all the time, that this is what I wish for. I don't usually know that I wish for this, but when it's around, when it's closer, it's clear that this is what I wish for: not to think about myself, but to be myself. I spend an awful lot of time, as I see now in retrospect, thinking about myself, talking, telling myself who I am, not *being* myself.

Dr. Welch:
Most of the talk about oneself is criticism of oneself, yes?

Same Person:
Yes, with some generosity, now and then.

Dr. Welch:
It is a struggle to accept that, because one believes in one's criticism. The struggle is not with the devil so much as it is with the subtlety of my distortion. It's very difficult to lose the judgment in accepting the manifestation.

Same Person:
It's true.

....

Fourth Questioner:
I've been thinking that for me the major issue is the difference between being present and not being present. I see that, in general, if I'm present, it doesn't happen because of me. It's not my will or my doing. Either it's due to circumstances, as in a meeting or the period of the thirteenth, when there are reminders and influences to help me be present, or it's some happenstance that, again, has nothing to do with me. Something like, as I think you once said, "money found in the street." It really isn't mine. Nevertheless, at least something in me values that, when it happens, even if I can't bring it about.

The one thing I do do is to sit, many mornings, and then, fairly reliably, there is more presence than there is the rest of the time. So, I guess there are two questions for me. One is that even though I appreciate being present—or part of me does—do I value it enough? And the second question relates to the fact that I drift away: for example, in a meeting when I fall asleep, or when I'm reacting, or when I get up from sitting and things happen. It seems to me that I lack an anchor—that what I need is an anchor to help me stay at that moment of presence.

Dr. Welch:
What is that anchor?

Same Person:
I haven't found one, so...

Dr. Welch:
If this anchor isn't one's relation to whatever it is we mean by attention, I would say it's rather difficult to ascertain what it might be. Is there some question in your mind about this?

Same Person:

I'm not sure I understand that, when you speak of a relation to attention. I guess I think of an anchor more as, for instance, one's sensation—of minding one's sensation.

Dr. Welch:

Yes. In the absence of attention?

Same Person:

Oh, no.

Dr. Welch:

Of course not. What is so complex about this? You know perfectly well that one's anchor with one's sensation is something that requires to be earned. It's something that, in the absence of a broken bone, is very difficult to obtain. Yes?

Same Person:

Yes.

Dr. Welch:

It seems so.

Third Questioner:

It seems to me that the part that wishes to figure things out is really not on the same scale as the one that begins to have a sense of understanding. There is a kind of connection that is actually interfered with by this annoying "What is this all about? Let me try to get this straight now."

Dr. Welch:

Yes. I think it might be of some interest, perhaps, to undertake to examine in oneself this question of struggle. Does it strike you as of some interest?

Same Person:
Well, it seems so now, in a way that it didn't before.

Dr. Welch:
It is something that Gurdjieff speaks about, again and again. It is certainly something that is on a level of inner engagement that seems full of pitfalls and mistaken tensions. And it is very clear that there is some aspect of struggle in this thing we speak about: accepting one's perception of oneself.

How does one deal with this faltering attention? What is a view of it in oneself that corresponds to what is and not to what I can inflame myself about? And what derives from that polarization, which is an aspect of struggle? Why should there be struggle? With whom?

Again, the magnitude of the undertaking is clear, and there is always the danger of misapprehension. Do we live on the level of something that can be properly called struggle?

Fifth Questioner:
I have difficulty facing this question because I'm afraid of it. Virtually every time the word "struggle" or "suffering" comes up, I shut it out. Something is afraid of it. And it strikes me that I don't discriminate between a bearable suffering and an unbearable one. I just lump it all together, and I want to avoid it. Why am I attracted to the Work in the first place? I'm running from suffering in some way, and yet it's also clear that there are times when I'm willing to undergo something.

Dr. Welch:
Whether one is willing to or not, one realizes that one suffers. It may not be the suffering of a saint, but one can suffer for the way one is. And the suffering is in relation to, at least, a vision of something that we have come to refer to as a "man without quotation marks." The characteristics of sleeping man become all too clear in one's experience, and one can suffer for all the wrong reasons. One doesn't necessarily suffer because of one's flawed capacities,

but rather there is the senseless suffering of the life of fear, of inner slavery, and considering—the things that one has brushed by or taken from quite another point of view.

Sixth Questioner:
I had the opportunity, last Sunday, to hear Terry Anderson speak. Terry Anderson is the journalist who was taken hostage in Beirut. He was there for seven years. This is someone who has really endured extraordinary physical suffering in his life. And the suffering that he spoke about was what he was forced to see about himself. And when people asked him how he felt about his captors, he said, "It's not about them; it's about what is in my heart."

Dr. Welch:
A very brave and true man. And it is very touching, isn't it, that he went beyond the place of covering it over in some way, or making it sound noble?

Same Person:
He said the journey was into himself and not about the external situation.

Dr. Welch:
Of course, there's no way to measure another man's suffering, but one can see that, if one's ego is exposed to oneself as the flattering idiot without guts and without a backbone, it can be devastating. And I suspect he probably had a lot of solitary, a lot of being abused, a lot of being turned into a nothing. And it's not an easy thing to be turned into a nothing. There has to be a sense of movement in relation to being turned into a nothing, because we avoid a great deal of that, but we come nearer to it than might otherwise be imagined.

Same Person:
And it struck me that we naturally run away from whatever little

sufferings we have, and he couldn't run away. There was no way to avoid looking into the mirror.

Dr. Welch:
That's right. No place to go.

Seventh Questioner:
It's a very helpful perspective for me. Because, if I think of how I usually am in my life, I'm either lost in my thought or I'm caught up in an emotional reaction. And if I try to be honest about the moments in which I could say that I feel alive, or closer to something that I would call reality, they are the moments when I tasted or experienced real feeling. Those feelings are either a taste of remorse, or a taste of aspiration, or of humility.

Most of those experiences come from being face to face with my ego, or having been exposed, and are moments of grace, not the result of my struggling. That seeing of my own nothingness, my dream being shattered, is transformed into something that is very precious, very real. And that's really where I want to be. But the reality of my life is that I'm fragmented: a little bit here, a little bit there, in one part or another part, and it's a just a circle of reaction. There is such a difference between that and the experiences of real feeling. They seem to be so far apart, and the connection seems to be so mysterious.

Dr. Welch:
Yes.

Same Person:
So, I don't know what to do. I think I know how to work. I go about it in a certain way, and that way may change from time to time. But I think, because of these experiences, a kind of faith has developed in my blundering, bumbling way of working. Because I know, somewhere, that I need to see what I don't see about myself.

Dr. Welch:
So, the direction is clear—which is the only thing that can ever be clear in any event.

So, the journey remains the destination.

Same Person:
I feel that something knows that it's a lot simpler than the way I go about it, the way I think about it.

Dr. Welch:
It's true.

Same Person:
And there's even an organic quality about that simplicity, but the way I'm constructed seems to conspire against that.

. . . .

Eighth Questioner:
What is an example of intentional suffering?

Dr. Welch:
Well, maybe you could be in a situation where you were quite sure that your habitual considering, your habitual nervousness, your traditional fear of being exposed for the fraud that you know very well you are, would be evoked. You can put yourself in a circumstance where you know very well that you will not find something grand and new, but rather some ancient fleabites that you could never quite easily deal with. So you put yourself into such a situation where you know, or are reasonably certain, that you're going to have this kind of response.

And you undertake to bring another kind of vision to what you know will be awakened in you, another quality of awareness. You make an effort to learn something about the quality and nature of your ordinary suffering.

Now, this is not suffering because of an acknowledged deficit of, let's say, attention. It's not because I think, "*Mea culpa.* I don't do it so good." But rather it's facing that from the point of view of what is required of a "man without quotation marks." And the absence of this is not my personal deficit, but the failure of my capacity to perceive my real obligation—very subtle and not so easy.

Gurdjieff says conscious labor, intentional suffering, and struggle are the three aspects of work without which there is no work. It's a terrible thing to quote scripture.

First Questioner:

I'd like to ask about what it could mean to be more actively engaged in my life. I feel that if anything has changed over the years of attempting some of this, it is that sometimes I can recognize when I'm more alive, or when there is more life in something as opposed to not, and when I'm receptive to that. Sometimes, in a piece of music, or in a story, or in a reading, there's a recognition of real life, and I'm very grateful for those moments, but I still feel very, very passive in the process. I feel sometimes there's a moment of recognition of that life in myself or in another person, but I don't find out how to create anything for myself, in myself, or how to be more actively engaged in life. Instead there's a very passive feeling.

Dr. Welch:

Yes, I know this thing you speak of. We've talked about aspects of this. Do I believe that I react when my buttons are pushed? Do I believe that I depend upon my exterior circumstances to move me? Do you believe that?

Same Person:

Well, sometimes. Sometimes I can't deny it.

Dr. Welch:

This is something that one is not instantly and always aware of. This is our state. And what is action as opposed to reaction? It is certainly possible to be aware of the absence, and sometimes, by engagement, to be aware of the possibility of something more nearly active. But to make an abstraction of it is a mistake, I think. There are occasions when it's apparent to me that I'm sleepwalking through my life again. This fact awakens in me. And I don't object to reaction. It's possible, in the midst of reaction, to see what is possible that is not just reaction. It may just be an active attitude toward it.

What is one's attitude? Does one have an attitude toward one's life? One has one, but does one see what it is? Your attitude toward your life is that you're passive, yes? Is that how you described it? Is that true? Not quite, is it?

Same Person:
That's not *all* of my attitude. A lot of my attitude is that I deserve to have great things in my life.

Dr. Welch:
You see the passivity in retrospect, not right now. Is that so?

Same Person:
I wouldn't say that, only. Because I would say there is a feeling of a yearning for something, and also a feeling that I have no idea what to do. There's a wish to approach life, and a wish to be alive. It's as if I have a little taste of it, but also that I feel very blocked from a deeper connection to life. From having had experiences of presence, in whatever conditions or situations, I hunger for more of that, and, at least, I have some recollection that it is possible to be in the midst of life and to have that connection to it. But most of the time I don't know how to be connected to that feeling of presence.

Dr. Welch:
Most of the time when you feel it, you don't know how it occurred, either.

Same Person:
That's right.

Dr. Welch:
They're the conditions in which you find yourself.

Same Person:
That's right. That's the passivity I'm talking about. Something occurs...

Dr. Welch:
Yes, but when you find yourself responsive in an active way, the conditions in which you're working are very different. Is that not so?

Same Person:
Are you talking about Work conditions?

Dr. Welch:
Well, yes, I'm talking about Work conditions, if you like. Because one cannot somehow just assert by fiat that one is going to have another attitude. One is evoked, you know. As the aphorism says, we can't help; we can only provide conditions. And in the presence of conditions that awaken something in you, where something can appear, you have quite another experience of that day's life, yes?

Same Person:
Yes, it's true, but...

Dr. Welch:
The same thing took place with the new baby, did it not?

Same Person:
Very much.

Dr. Welch:
There was another condition. You were awakened with a concern that you could not be *inactive* about. Isn't that so?

Same Person:
Yes, that's true.

Dr. Welch:
And you had no complaint then. In both cases it was conditions.

Same Person:
But this can also occur in the ordinary conditions of my daily life.

Dr. Welch:
What's so ordinary about the conditions of your daily life? [laughter]

Same Person:
Well, that's the point, in a way. I lose the contact with the sense of the magic in everyday life. And it's there, I know it's there, but the perception of magic in everyday life seems to come upon me accidentally. I don't know. Maybe what I'm saying is that I wish to be independent of conditions, and maybe that's ridiculous.

Dr. Welch:
Well, I don't know that it's ridiculous, and I don't know that you mean to be independent of them. But I think it's an extraordinary illumination to discover that there are conditions in which something appears in you, or something is activated in you, that you can't seem to assert otherwise. Is that so?

Same Person:
Yes, it is so.

Dr. Welch:
It seems to me it is. And you say, "Well, how can I see?" or "How can I respond in a positive way to conditions that vary from these?" Maybe I can't. Maybe I just have to seek these other conditions for a longer period. I know very well what conditions will produce certain things in me.

Same Person:

I think I don't understand what conditions are, really.

Dr. Welch:

Yes, you do. "When two or three are gathered together, in my name..."[1] When surrounded by others that are like-minded, I remember my reason for being there. And something appears that isn't readily described. Isn't that recognizable?

Same Person:

I think it is recognizable, but...

Dr. Welch:

Don't you think you recognize it?

Same Person:

But, you see, that's part of my question. I feel that I recognize it when it occurs, but I don't understand my part in it or in the recognition. So I end up feeling dependent.

Dr. Welch:

I'm not at all sure that anybody necessarily recognizes their part. One is not coming to these conditions as a bundle of wisdom; one comes to these conditions with a question. Something may or may not occur, but if it does, it's a kind of magic that takes place, and there is a beam of understanding that corresponds to another level of concern in me. But I can't pretend that there is some way in which I can manipulate this. It isn't the shortest distance between two points. And I acknowledge that I don't understand, with any certainty, what the conditions are in which I experience another level of awareness of myself, one that evokes another attitude, another point of application. Indeed, I even possibly recognize that at this moment I wake up to what my condition *is*. Is that not so? Yes and no?

1   From Matthew 18:20 "For where two or three are gathered together in my name, there am I in the midst of them."

Same Person:
[laughing] That's right.

Second Questioner:
It struck me, in thinking about the nature of struggle, about the nature of the effort that we wish to understand, that it's a little bit analogous to a situation where I'm trying to remember somebody's name, and I can't remember it. In a sense, I'm trying to do something. But when this name comes to me, I must say that it doesn't really give the impression of something that I did. And it struck me this evening, when I was washing the dishes, that it was somewhat the same thing. In doing ordinary things my attention comes and goes. But when I felt more alive, when I felt as though I was actually *in* my body, with the sensation of my arm, it was as though it was a familiar experience remembered again, but not done by me. In a way, it's more like trying to remember something that I've forgotten, something that can be given to me again, because it does always seem to be something that's given, rather than taken.

Dr. Welch:
[after a pause] Who struggles?

Same Person:
I don't think that I can claim to do that. But when it is given to me, I can be aware that there is now something that can be forgotten. I mean, sometimes, one even starts to worry—then probably it has already changed. And it struck me, too, in this, that Mme de Salzmann used to say that it requires a very strong attention. That's a question. What does that mean?

Dr. Welch:
What does that mean, a very strong attention? That reminds me that Gurdjieff says that only super-effort counts. Well, we're not hard on ourselves in that way, but at the same time, this is a haunting recollection, and the memory of this is very thin. What

is missing? It seems to me that we're back to the quality of feeling—that I'm at the wrong place in myself. I can't bring myself to the recognition of the true situation of how I am. I want to repair it here, fix it there. But I've forgotten—if I remember the work at all—the scale on which it exists, and I'm personally dissatisfied, but for the wrong reasons. I'm personally dissatisfied because I'm uncomfortable with this image of myself. But I'm not touched by organic shame that my life is wasted, and I don't take into account what the real lack is.

So, I know that I don't find anything by tugging at the feeling or tugging at the head when my only concern is whether I'm comfortable or not, disappointed or not. And what is an avenue to self-awareness, which is clearly absent when I'm in this state?

Third Questioner:
I also have a question about struggle. The struggle we talk about almost seems like it's a bigger thing than I've ever experienced, but, nevertheless, I was in a situation where circumstances caused an internal struggle in me. My father had one very strong idea about something he wanted me to be doing. My brother had another very strong idea about what he thought I should be doing. And my wife had a third idea, also very strong, about what I should be doing. I don't notice this very often, but, clearly, I spend a lot of my life trying to make everybody happy and doing what I think they want me to be doing. And I was in a situation where it was impossible for me to feel that I was satisfying all of these diverse demands, whether real or imagined. So there was conflict in me, and I can't really say I did anything with it, but I did try to be in front of it.

I had an image that I seemed to return to a lot, which is from *The Odyssey*, where Odysseus has arranged to have himself tied to the mast. And something of that was the feeling I had, that I felt a pull in several directions, and could go nowhere, and could only stay, as best I could. This had a tendency to move, in my thoughts, in a direction toward depression, a deflation of my normal sense of myself. Things seemed bleak. I couldn't make a number of people happy, and I felt the world was not measuring up to the way I wanted it to be. So a downward movement, in a sense, was taking place in me. But I wanted to try to stay in front of that, even though it wasn't at all a pleasant direction.

And then I went to the sitting tonight, in the midst of these feelings. And one thing that stood out in my mind in the sitting was that there's an awful lot of energy devoted to positing that I know what I'm doing, that I know how to try, that I know what I'm attempting to do in my personal work. Perhaps because of this sort of weakening of my ego, if that's what it was, I was more inclined to say, "I really don't know at all what I'm about. I don't know how to try. If anything is going to take place, he'll have to do it, or whatever in me is the highest part of me." I didn't have the capacity. "Thy will and not my will" seemed to be the only direction at that moment. When that idea crossed my mind, it seemed that an immediate change in my state took place. In a way, something was coming together that before was being held apart by my constant struggle to achieve something, to know what I'm doing, to control the process.

The Work often says that one needs a strong ego, and I'm not really sure what that means in the context of this experience. Something was trying to stay in front of this, and that required a certain fortitude of some kind. But what I associate with the word "ego" felt very dampened in this, and yet that seemed to facilitate something.

Dr. Welch:
I thought it was fascinating when you pointed out something that so many people have experienced only after a good deal of such "doing": that they're always undertaking to please somebody else. They wish to be approved, in a sense, or maybe loved, or maybe admired in various ways that will please people who are near and dear to them. And whole careers get woven around this, which often only becomes clear after the fact. And that's essentially what you said about this triad of opposites that were confronting you by way of your father, and your brother and your wife. Yes?

Same Person:
Yes.

Dr. Welch:
It seems to me that the place where something could be seen would be just there, this business of pleasing the devils of our life—set them up and win their approval. At some point you were able to give up, to separate yourself from this triad of victimization, really. It seems to me that you stopped struggling at a certain point, and the struggle was a futile one, because it was over something quite without substantive motivation. Then you came to a place where you found yourself to be, in a sense, relieved, because you were no longer trying to put square plugs into round holes. Am I wrong about this? Didn't you come to a place of relief?

Same Person:
I did, but I have a question about that. It doesn't seem to be just that I saw that there is this engine that is literally constantly seeking approval, or love, or whatever. What often seems to happen to me is that I turn that into a label. I say, "Oh, that's that." The seeing—that sometimes feels so freeing—is really a big thing. I mean, if it happens for a moment, that's really quite wonderful, but to sustain it is beyond my capacity.

There was something about this experience where I was given no choice but to be stuck in this uncomfortable place. And that friction seemed to be a right place to be. But I'm very cautious about saying even that, because then I turn that into something that I try to use as an achievement mechanism. I'm constantly trying to figure out how to do this, and perhaps the biggest thing about all this was that somehow I was confronted with the feeling that I had no idea where to go—feeling very lost, actually. But there's also this feeling that some part isn't lost. I feel a certain confidence about that, and it isn't the ordinary part, but there's some part that feels solid. But I never really give it a chance, and I don't even know how to give it a chance.

Dr. Welch:

That last observation suggests that you have some image, perhaps, or notion that you're in charge, that you're running the show. Do you believe you are?

Same Person:

I don't believe it in our conversation right now, but I usually have a very powerful feeling that I have that sense of control.

Dr. Welch:

It's true. Events move us more than we move ourselves. And our notions of management are difficult to verify and very misleading. It seems to me that you arrived at the place where you simply dropped this. Am I right?

Same Person:

Yes, you're right. But it wasn't like I just went away; I turned my attention in a certain inner direction that I normally don't. So it wasn't just a dropping, it was also a looking in another place, somehow.

Dr. Welch:

From another place? From a higher place?

Same Person:

I may not be understanding you, but it seemed to me that I wasn't actually looking *from* a higher place. I was looking from a lower place than usual, and I was looking up, internally, and I think I don't do that very often.

Dr. Welch:

That's another way of saying, from my point of view, "a look from above." It was a look from another place in you, a look toward objectivity, if you like: seeing the emptiness of your plans from this other place, seeing it rather than being lost in it. Is that not it? Weren't you trying to see it?

Same Person:
Hmmm. I think there may have been a seeing, but...

Dr. Welch:
It wasn't as intentional as all that.

Same Person:
No, unfortunately, it wasn't. There was still a lot of "me" in this. I left a position where I thought I knew what I was doing. And therefore the question arose, "Does something in me know? Because I don't." There's a line from one of the essays of Emerson that I was reading this week, just a brief line: "We are wiser than we know." And somehow there seemed to be some wisdom in me that I don't control.

Fourth Questioner:
I'm remembering circumstances where I was put in a difficult situation. And I may not notice it at the time, but there's comes a point where I actually look for help. It's as if I've given up this untenable position, and now am somehow open to receiving help. The image I have is that the help is just above my eyes, and I never raise my head high enough to notice it. Until, finally, I do.

Dr. Welch:
I think there's something in what you say. One comes to a place where one is open to the reality of a situation that I cannot help, and I need help. And it doesn't mean that then everything clears, because it doesn't necessarily, but it's at a place of relative slowing, if not stopping, of a certain kind of futile agitation about an impossible, irresolvable problem. From that level there's no way of resolving it, of reconciling it.

But I'm still struck by that recognition of pleasing someone with *my* perceived image. There's something so touchingly true that one always seeks a measure that one cannot determine, in an internal way, for oneself. And one can't settle for this, but one will act on it.

Fifth Questioner:
I have a question about doing and struggle, and what my part is. I've been experimenting with a certain way that I am, and it feels like a right experiment. And although it could be an attempt to re-form, it feels more like a new possibility. Almost every day there's a point at which, as people might sometimes say, I know I'm going to lose it. I'm just going to become internally distraught or upset. If I hear something, for example, something that makes me feel that the kids aren't really very smart, or they get a low grade at school, or something, this all starts coming up. What I've been trying is just to kind of refuse that, not to become involved in it, not to let it just take me over. And it's hard, and it isn't *really* possible, but it feels like a new way of trying to...to *be*. Because, otherwise, when my head is telling me that there's nothing in that, it doesn't seem to solve anything; it never makes a difference with the situation. The emotional anxiety that comes over me doesn't seem to help, so it's helpful to try to not let it take over.

Dr. Welch:
If I follow you, I would say that you are undertaking to prevent a pattern of fear and self-destruction. Is that too exaggerated? Is it that? Is something in you destroyed in this way? If it goes on, it has its beginning, and its middle, and then its final end, but it has its way?

Same Person:
I think it's a habit I've had of just getting very upset internally about things that are not really a big thing.

Dr. Welch:
It seems to me that this is something to embrace, not to under-take to stop. Do you know what I mean by that?

Same Person:
I do, but I think that's what I'm trying...

Dr. Welch:
It's doesn't sound to me as though you are. You're trying to stop it.

Same Person:
I'm trying to not let it take me over.

Dr. Welch:
Let it take you over, but see where it takes you. Not just to fear, but to what fear? To *what* are you descending? Where are you really going? Do you see the fear? Where is it? What is it of, ultimately? Where does it go?

Can you just face that, instead of undertaking to prevent it? Does that seem like an impossible effort?

Do you know it well? Do you see it well?

Same Person:
It's the words that I think are mixing me up. What I try is to feel it in sensation, and not to think about what it is, when it begins. So, when you say, "know it well," I don't know. I try to stay out of my head, because, if I'm in my head with the thoughts, then that's when I just get lost in it. But if I try to just see what's happening in my sensation of it, then it's a different experience.

Dr. Welch:
Well, you know, there are those who would say, about a pattern of disordered fear of this kind, "Step away from this, and move to another place in yourself." Not so easy. Nonetheless, this is another point of view. But I think you need to try to experience what it is, because you can be absolutely sure that these are stinking little devils, not your spiritual death. This is a pattern, an old pattern of response, that has its roots in God knows what, but should be seen for what, in fact, it purports to convey to you. And I wouldn't say it shouldn't be in the head, it shouldn't be here, it shouldn't be there. Your head, and your heart, and your body... You have to be present to see this. You're not to be taken away. You have to sense yourself; you have to be in yourself. You have

to be active in this if you wish to undertake to, as the expression goes, "embrace it," and damn well familiarize yourself with it. It's not God's hand striking you down.

But you don't think it is anyway, do you?

Same Person:
No. No, I didn't think so.

Dr. Welch:
This is not something new. This is something ancient, isn't it?

Same Person:
Yes. But it's me. It's part of my life. It's the way I am. It's me. It happens all the time.

Dr. Welch:
Yes. Well, there's nothing easy about how to approach it, but another way to approach it is to simply move from that place in oneself by an active effort, and devote some attention elsewhere. Not so easy. But again, one moves oneself to another scale and sees this for what it is, which is a piece of imagination, probably mixed with considering, and mixed with all kinds of things. But it's a pattern that is so familiar that one is tempted to believe that one has to submit to it. There's such a thing as jujitsu, you know.

Same Person:
There is one interesting thing that's happened, when I've been like this over things that happened at school—in my political life there. I've realized that part of it, in that context, is because I believe that I'm actually right about whatever it is I'm upset about. This has a certain hold on me, but because I'm trying not to get carried away with it or lost, I realize I may *not* be right. They may be right. It was quite interesting because I really always assume, in a very childish way, that I probably know better than this poor guy who has been struggling to be a good headmaster of the

school for ten years—that little old me really knows the better thing to do.

Dr. Welch:
You have the choice to undertake to really see this for what it is, or to undertake to move to another world in yourself, and simply recognize that whatever this is, it certainly is in the field of imaginary confrontations and conflicts. It's a reaction to the fear of outer darkness, yes?

Same Person:
I don't know. The main feature of it is some point at which—I don't know how to say it, but I don't expect that this is unfamiliar to many women—anyway, the point at which you just sort of become irrational. I don't know. [laughing]

Dr. Welch:
It's better than becoming rational, isn't it?

Same Person:
Somebody asks me for something when I'm in the middle of something, and I'm really busy, and suddenly, I'm gone, in a certain way. And it seems as though there's a point at which I can say in the moment, "No, I'm not going to do that." But it's difficult. It's not easy, and that's why there's a question. I feel as though I'm doing something. I know we're told that this perception of things won't help. I know that to be true, but, in this case, it feels like something that I have to try to choose.

Dr. Welch:
You have to try to see it. Or you have to try to divert your attention to something more serious, more your concern, more in the realm where you have the opportunity to be present to yourself. Not so easy, in the midst of the turmoil of the day, but this is the alternative to being immobilized by it.

First Questioner:
There is a question that arose in me this week about the question
that Mme de Salzmann used to raise: "So, how to be?"

Dr. Welch:
Not "What to do?"

Same Person:
And the question arose, somehow, in connection with another
question, which is about what I know, or think I know, and from
where in me do I have that impression that I know something.

I have the sense that I customarily act as if I know what I'm
trying to do. It's a presumption that is there before I venture in
any direction. Even if I'm saying to myself that I don't know, I
seem to think I know how to seek. I wonder whether this assertion of an effort to know from a certain place in myself is actually
an aspect of my sleep, an aspect of my blindness. When I think I'm
successful at it, I actually aggrandize myself in that arena. And
when I'm less successful at it, I rationalize it, and brush myself off,
and immediately try again—always from this assumption that I
know what I'm about.

This has raised the question of whether there is a "knower"
in me that truly knows, that already knows what I need. And
this ties in with this notion of how to be, because in exploring
that question, without trying to answer it, impressions arise in
me that give the sense that there is something in me that knows,
though I'm not at the center of that knowing. It's an impression
that seems quite real to me: that there is an intelligence that is

denied the opportunity to function, because I'm constantly asserting a kind of false knowing.

Dr. Welch:

It is true that we have these intuitive punches that seem to be fostered by the words that we know so well in our heads. And the practice of Gurdjieff's point of view and the philosophy of his point of view are separated by a gulf. It's very difficult not to be impressed by the gulf between one's aspiration and one's manifestation.

It seems to me that, at this place in oneself, one can go on in this quasi-self-awareness, or one can turn to some practical inner movement that one knows something about. It isn't a largely complicated thing to say to myself, "I am dispersed. I'm scattered. I don't see that I am scattered. I'm lost in my scatteredness." I don't see it. I talk as though I see it, but I don't see it clearly, in the way that I see it when I'm in a circumstance where I'm not identified with my own manifestation.

And so we go back to square one. We think of ourselves as experienced old hands who know the way. And even when we see that we don't know the way, we're far from square one. But it seems to me that in this work we are always beginning. We're filled with the recollections of our triumphs and our failures— our self-evaluations, which are very nicely laid out as: "I see my passivity. Well, I don't quite see it, but I'm not unaware of it. And I wish to be comfortable. And there is a division in me. I am 'yes' and 'no.'"

What is the possibility? What does it mean when Mme de Salzmann says, "Now the question is there: How to be?" Well, one knows something about the words "How to be." One is also not entirely without a point of initiation of some connection with oneself. What is the vulnerable place in my economy, in my totality? Can I get at my head? Can I get at my heart? Can I get at my body? What can I get at? Where can I establish another inner connection with myself? What do I undertake under such circumstances? Apart from saying, "Well, tomorrow I'll try again."

What does it mean to undertake to have an action on myself? I'm not talking about succeeding at something, but I'm talking about just getting into a more nearly real inner relationship with myself that I'm not unfamiliar with, but haven't sought under these circumstances. What can I do? And this will reflect how I can be.

Are you content to sit in this mud puddle? What is the role of whatever fragment of will one has, assuming that one does indeed bear a wish? We talk about our wish. What do we mean by our wish? What is the nature of the barrier that we continue to be confronted by?

Second Questioner:
I don't know if it's precisely what you're speaking about, but it seems to me that, at different times, different parts of myself are in relationship. Sometimes my heart is open, and I can sense that I feel something, and that it's real. Or sometimes, I can sit quietly and maybe have a different sense of my mind. Or I can do some hard physical work and really feel the presence of my body. Usually I'm either unaware of my body, or, at best, I'm aware that it's not right, that something's missing. I often have a sense that something's lacking. It's rare that all these things happen simultaneously. Rather it seems as though it's just little pieces. Is that close to what you're talking about? I have a question about the development of a human being over the course of their life.

Dr. Welch:
Well, we're talking about *now*.

I'm very important to myself now. I've been describing my inner conflicts. I haven't really weighed very carefully the scale on which I see myself, but somehow it's a little suspicious. I don't see the helplessness I am confronting and trying to articulate. I'm not speaking about my capacity, now. I'm speaking about the difficulties that I encounter, which do not correspond to my occasional picture of myself as a spiritual warrior. And I'm not at the place where I can, in an objective way—or even in an approximate, nearly objective way—see my nothingness. I haven't thought about that much. It hasn't been broken open in this little concern with the "unableness" that we all speak about on occasion. We don't know what we don't know. Now, as old China hands in the Work—you've been around for a long time—what, in fact, takes place with this state that you've described? Where is it now? Still being pushed uphill?

Third Questioner:
What you said evoked for me a very strong thought, and it just felt that what I do is substitute one image for another, or, in a way, one dream for another. I've been feeling very strongly this week that there are certain things that I know I need to do in my life, practical things. I come back, again and again, to the idea that if I can't face and take care of these practical things in my life—things that are at the level of an *obyvatel*—then I can't take anything else on in any other imaginary or non-imaginary realm. Somehow, that's connected for me, because it really struck me when you talked about being more conscious, seeing a bit more, and how seductive that is. I think I'm doing something, or even know I'm not doing something, but somehow there's a certain rhythm that keeps me there, and I can't get beyond that.

Dr. Welch:
Yes. The magnitude of the undertaking from this point of view cannot be exaggerated. One is not dealing with a simple manipulation. One's undertaking of this is barricaded by a conditioned lifetime of, as you say, seeking comfort. One comes up against the one who is going with the current. This is a reality of people's lives.

First Questioner:
I've become interested in an aspect of negativity, a sort of mi-
nor-league anger that I carry around with me a lot of the time. I
don't think it's very special. I think a lot of people have it. But it's
striking in comparison to how I am after an extended period of
work, which I would label as being quite positive and...

Dr. Welch:
Tolerant.

Same Person:
...and tolerant. I think this kind of anger at others is often a little
bit objective, but there also is an element of imaginary envy, which
really has no basis. At one point, about a week ago, I got a slight
glimmer of that, and it almost immediately changed my attitude. I
think this envy is a kind of emotional imagination, because I know
very well, at least theoretically, that we're all really pretty much
in the same situation. The emotional envy translates into a kind of
anger. For example, I'm working around here, and I start getting
angry at everybody who has left things lying around or whatnot.

Dr. Welch:
It puts me in mind of Mme de Salzmann's words in that reading
we heard the other day in which she spoke about comparing oneself. Is that the kind of thing you mean?

Same Person:
I don't remember that aspect of the reading, Dr. Welch.

Dr. Welch:
Well, she spoke about the variety of ways in which one protected the egotistical self.

Same Person:
Yes, I think that is what I'm talking about. Although I don't see that protection, if that's what it is, very clearly. I don't perceive it as a protection, it's perceived as a... Well, it's not perceived very well at all.

Dr. Welch:
There is a whole range of defense mechanisms that I really haven't heard or thought about very much. I compare myself with others and see their circumstances as more full of ease than hardship, or full of other advantages in life, in one way or another. But it seems to me that it has some relation to the intensity with which one enfolds oneself—without question—in this state. It's something that's not very clear and is very, very difficult to discern, but it's an aspect of the basis for an attitude that one has. It's the distortion of one's own protective attitude toward the inner image of oneself, which is not at all tolerant of others. Is that how you see it?

Same Person:
I think that is a generalization of what I see.

Dr. Welch:
Does it result in any violence? Overt violence?

Same Person:
Oh, no. I mean if somebody calls, I'm all sunshine and roses. And I feel that way too. It's kind of interrupted. I don't mean I always have this, but it's one aspect of my slavery, or my occasional slavery.

Dr. Welch:
It's a strange thing, negativity, a very strange thing, because it's

all internal. One doesn't recognize that it's *never* related so much to others as it's related to oneself.

Same Person:
That's true. That's what I think I saw the other day, that there was the envy. And the seeing almost immediately released something. Also, there's a subtlety to it, because it's partly that my wandering mind allows it room. If I have some awareness of myself, then something else takes over, and this doesn't have room.

Dr. Welch:
It's a very strange thing, when one stands apart from it, personally, for a moment, when one isn't beleaguered by it. When one knows the opposite, one is then in a very different place in oneself, where this is really absent, and one is quite free, or relatively free of it.

The other side of it is that I don't think of it as a reflection of my level of being, but rather I'm justifying all kinds of things with my circuitous inner mischief. I'm victimized by this aspect of self. In a sense, I'm shoring myself up in the face of this kind of competitive negativity. And it has nothing to do with reality, in all likelihood. Or if it does have some echo of something that has been part of an exchange, it's not something of substantive materiality. It is a kind of self-indulgence, because one feels very self-righteous about this while it's active. It's an example of the inner slavery that occupies so much of one's hours and one's days—if it turns itself on.

And who turns it on? Why does it come up? What is the twisted inner logic that makes it significant? This would be said to be a psychological aspect of the Work. Well, it's not so much psychological as it is the life of the automatism. It's the unattended life. Even though I would say I was concentrating on it, it isn't so. It is occupying me, and I have left myself unattended. And I don't see that, except maybe sometimes. But certainly not while it's having its way with me. It's part of the suffering of the human situation.

It is very difficult to perceive that this kind of thing has a life of its own, that it preoccupies one and leaves one in such a way that one doesn't see that one is no longer there and no longer attending to one's life. The unattended occupant of the carriage is being manipulated by its own automatism. And it is rooted in the ego.

This is always a reflection of being, not of something else. And it is such a contrast when one, by the grace of God, is elevated to some extent and experiences freedom and a feeling of meaning. And it's astounding that it has no certain recurrence by intention.

Second Questioner:
I had a similar thing happen this week in which I had to remove myself from a situation that I felt was dangerous, and someone else had to jump in. And I was very upset for a few hours, because I thought it was dangerous, but when I finally asked myself why I was still churning about this, I realized that, underneath all that, I was upset that I would be not be perceived as a trooper, as a great person. And there was an awful lot, even under that, of being afraid that I would be compared in a way that I felt was not...

Dr. Welch:
...sufficiently glorified.

Same Person:
Yes. It reminded me of what you always say, that if you keep uncovering the layers, you find a deeper layer of considering.

Dr. Welch:
Yes, particularly when I'm quite sure I'm behaving on a question of principle. One cannot excuse what one finds because it's a reflection of being, but as one goes further, it seems to me that the fact is reasserted that one is in the grip of nature. One is not, so to speak, embracing nature. Nature has me by the throat.

The whole thing is such a travesty of imaginary wandering, all the time with the curious attraction that I have to the idea of somehow protecting myself from being seen for what I privately suspect is my array of deficits, my array of flaws. I don't acknowledge this. I don't like to acknowledge it, in any event.

But one can always turn from that to the place where one is released, and there is such a change, such a difference. It always seems to me that one comes to the place of real meaning, not this imaginary world of outrageous slings and arrows.

Third Questioner:
When you give up that imaginary world, you also have to give up the illusion that you're controlling the situation, and I think that's one of the hardest things. But it can be very freeing, once you're over the cliff.

Dr. Welch:
I think one needs to see how deeply this is encrusted in one, and how stabilized one is in whatever level one occupies. It's a real movement that relieves one from this, not some kind of wrenching, or reforming, or undoing something, but simply moving into a place in oneself that is relatively apart from that preoccupied space.

I suppose that this is why one can find certain aspects about this work that seem to be therapeutic. But if one seeks it because it's therapeutic, it is a mistake, because the need for therapy disappears in this inner movement away from preoccupation. It's not necessary. It's part of the absurdity of one's reactions in this murky soup of self-evasion.

But it is true that one gives altogether too much of one's life to this, and one isn't so out of love with it as one thinks. How does one get so attached to these self-preoccupied daydreams? One may not welcome them, but, nonetheless, one entertains them with a great deal more enthusiasm than one would wish to acknowledge, even to oneself. And their power is very great.

Fourth Questioner:
From what you're saying, I feel that things like anger feel good because they are affirmations of myself, in the absence of a real affirmation of myself. If I see the process a little bit, or if I see myself becoming lost, or if I become curious about it, then I'm in touch with the mystery and the not-knowing of who I am. Then, it

seems to me, there is a feeling of meaning, which has a power of its own. It is the kind of affirmation of being alive that I wish for. So, for me, the question becomes how to stay in touch with the sense of mystery that comes when I recognize that I don't know myself. The recognition can come—even if I am doing something habitual, like being lost in anger for the ten thousandth time—if I can find an opening where I don't insist that I know who I am in that moment. So, all my questions seem to boil down to how do I keep trying to stay in touch with the mystery of being alive.

Dr. Welch:
I was interested in your touching upon the ridiculous negative affirmation of anger in oneself that is poised with a curious self-righteousness. And it's very interesting that it's the only affirmation that some people have in which they can feel a kind of fulfillment. They're in a position that's unassailable in this ridiculous business, and it takes a lot of grace to get out of that state and to be in touch with quite another affirmation. Certainly it helps to know the enlivening, activating sense of the situation, which is not one of knowing, but one of not-knowing.

Same Person:
Would you agree that anger is just one example of the many ways that the ego makes itself into the master of the universe? For example, I can be depressed, but that's taking myself very seriously, and there's a thrill in depression, too. It's the same kind of affirmation. I know who I am when I'm depressed. I know who I am when I'm furious. I know who I am when I'm lost in all of these different ego-affirming states. It seems to me we've been told in many ways that, unless there is a master of some kind, then the ego takes control. And if there's a place for something else to come in, of a different nature, then the ego can take its rightful place. But I see that I really don't understand that.

Dr. Welch:
One has a recurring pattern of responding to certain aspects of

life with this self-protective violence of one sort or another. It is a kind of upside-down affirmation of the importance of this, and the need to husband it. It's curiously self-destructive in its way, and, as Ouspensky used to say, "The only thing you have to sacrifice in this work is your suffering," as if it were something that one could just give up. But I think it's an interesting statement. If to sacrifice is to make sacred, one realizes that one is dealing with a larger undertaking than perhaps it sounds like. The great clinker in one's life, the real stick-in-the-spokes, is suffering. And then it is said, a bit jocularly, and perhaps with a raised eyebrow, that it's the only thing you have to give up, the only sacrifice you have to make.

It's always a little upsetting to hear that one's negativity is something that one actually loves. The replication of the same old nonsense that recurs and returns is obviously not at all related to anything substantive and real. So, we have recognizable patterns, in that way. And one begins to get in touch with some things in oneself that one doesn't necessarily welcome, but can't avoid. One knows very well, I think, after some time with this undertaking, that one is not only repetitive about this, but also surprisingly reactive and responsive to these repetitious patterns of behavior. One would think that this would begin to seem so fruitless that one would not be so devoted to them. But there it is; it recurs.

. . . .

One thing that I can recognize is that it is nonsense to think I know why somebody else is doing something in relation to *me*. He's just as helpless as I am, and he's doing whatever he's doing from his own pattern. He is not doing anything because of *my* need for some kind of tolerance or, indeed, something more than tolerance, something devoted and flattering. It seems to me that the dances that we do around these campfires of feeling are always patterned and drearily similar, which is one of the saddest things about it all. One has this tired old trooper with his same old mishmash, which is always repeating itself, and having its way with a driven psyche. And that psyche is simply one that is unattended. There's nobody there. Nobody's present to this, so that it behaves in a way that is a tired melodrama of what is called the human condition. It's not a bounding awakening of activation, on the basis of a great sense of passion about something. It's this tired little old love of oneself and the constant nonsense that one is not being taken into account enough.

First Questioner:
When the mind is actually not quite automatic about this, but when it has a more objective thought, that feels more uncomfortable at first. Instead of the mind just going right along with it, there is a kind of suffering to see that this is not corresponding. That may not be the mind and heart working together, but it is at least, in a sense, on the road to freedom.

Dr. Welch:
Exactly. Maybe this is in the realm of "being-reason"—something that is a capacity of a mind that isn't entirely throttled by the smoke from our fire. I'm not sure that it's clear to me, but it does seem that there's a higher mind. Maybe it is not exactly a "look from above," but one makes some kind of effort to perceive what it is in reality—what its "*is-ness*" is. Then one awakens to an association that is not a cheap thing. One is reminded that there is a circumstance that one doesn't usually perceive. There is a past that one can recollect, and there is an awful recognition of the pattern. Very reasonably one can come to a place of freedom from this kind of ridiculous suction.

Fifth Questioner:
It seems to me that part of the addictive or attractive nature of my ordinary state is that the emotions are very powerful, and my emotions are actually connected with my mind in the wrong way. I'm thinking thoughts that correspond to what is, almost invariably, a very childish emotion. My thought has been taken by this. So I could, in a particular situation that had a brief little reaction, go on

thinking about it for half an hour, turning it over again—the same old garbage. I'm annoyed, and I'm feeling very justified, and I'm thinking in a way that is exactly in line with that. Of course it's nonsense, but, as you say, it's unattended. There's really nobody there.

Dr. Welch:
That's the reality of it, I think.

You will recall that very effective account from Gurdjieff of the man whose day is recorded. The ending of it is, "I could go on with this picture of your day—you free man!" This is the description of the characteristic manifestations of all the little events of someone's life—the way in which flattery works, the way in which considering acts, the way in which one preens oneself and one is suddenly jolted. One has all these ridiculous ways of living, at the expense of inner valuation—constantly the victim of external valuation. Another man's valuation is immediately accepted, instead of being heard and being judged against one's own inner value.

. . . .

So one is always victimized by the glint in some stranger's eye. One can be crushed by a relative stranger, who, with an acute gesture or word or expression, judges us as being a nothing. And this "nothing" makes us suffer. We're not at the place where we have our own measure, where we could look at such an assault and say, "Well, he must have had a bad breakfast. It's his problem. This doesn't correspond to what I know about myself."

And it would seem ridiculous to say, "Well, we have to get this information, because otherwise we don't know how to deal with what we perceive to be the judgments of the world." That's ridiculous, you know. Self-knowledge is not for that purpose. It's something that is a base from which one can begin to practice the art of being alive, and to move into a circumstance that has nourishment, instead of being the victim of every perceived absence of respect for an ego that one devote's one's energies to protecting.

Dr. Welch:

After the serpent and Eve and Adam had filled their roles, God apparently spoke and said, "Adam, where are you?"[1] The fundamentalists wondered why, if He could see everything, He couldn't answer that Himself. And others turned to the question of "Where are you now?"—not to find him, but for him to ask himself where he was, now. Wonderful question: "Where are we now?"

First Questioner:

There's something that I am seeing, sometimes, which is that I'm not open, in some way. And it's the same for me now, which is why I want to speak. It's almost as if there's something in me, in many situations, where I just want to leave—not necessarily physically—but there's something that is not willing to be more fully there.

I saw it today, when I was with my friend, and *wishing* to be there. And I don't know what it is, clearly. But I have the taste sometimes, and the feeling, that everything would be so different if, in any given circumstance, I would just accept to be there, whatever that meant. Not in any fancy way, but just accept that this was how this five minutes was going to be, or this was how my afternoon was going to be. But there is something—it could even be just a laziness—a sort of a feeling, not really that I just want to go home and put my feet up and be on my own, but something like that. Maybe it's *my* nature that I don't always want to

1   The Welches had recently been reading *Genesis* from the bible with a small group of people.

engage with a situation or with other people. I'm trying to explore it as I'm saying it. Part of me just wants to retreat and be on
my own. But I think that's most of my life. And I'm interested now
to see what that is.

Dr. Welch:
I don't know that one so much awakens to a *response* to "Where
are you now, Adam?" One can readily accept this as a question that
Adam can understand to ask himself, rather than to imagine that
he was hiding. But it raises the next question, in a way, from that
assertion of Gurdjieff that, as he put it, "You," meaning each one of
us, "are not who you think you are," which is another difficult one.
Because I am not necessarily so aware of what I think I am, but
the question requires me to observe how I am, how I move, what
the pattern of my intention is, and how close my intention is to
who I think I am, or who I am. These further questions are evoked
when "Where are you now?" becomes clear. It is something difficult to be certain about, except by the grace of God.

Same Person:
Hiding is a good word, actually, because that's almost the feeling
I had today—that I was kind of trying to hide from something.

Dr. Welch:
Yes.

Under the influence of the wise serpent—not the devil, not
the evil sign—but the one who seemed to clarify things, for a moment, in that very confusing story.

Second Questioner:
I have an impression of myself that is both gratifying in a certain
way, and disturbing in another. It's gratifying because I think I
am seeing something, but it's disturbing because what I see is uncomfortable. It began in the sitting earlier this evening, where I
could almost palpably taste that something was missing. And that

something was *me*, somehow. There was this clear impression that I was able to see myself, and I was seeing myself, but what I was seeing was the absence of something. It made me think of self-remembering and self-observation. The difference between these has always puzzled me, somewhat. My impression tonight was that I was observing myself, but that I was not remembering myself—that there was something more central that was not collected by this inner sight on myself.

I contrast this to an experience I had in Movements, earlier this week, when there was something there: there was a sense of myself. And tonight what I can see of it is that I am, in a way, scattered and only interested on the outside: "What are the impressions others have of me?" That isn't even really so much the center of it; there doesn't appear to be a center. And there's nothing I can do about it, which feels, in a way, honest. I see that I have no idea how to correct this—what seems to be a true deficiency. So, it's uncomfortable, but it seems to be a fact about myself.

Dr. Welch:
Well, it's interesting that, perhaps, you were more moved by the disappointment, as you describe it, of the absence of something, than by making an effort to accept this absence. Who was disappointed in the absence of something? There was an observer who has an array of dissatisfactions with this, saying that this is somehow incomplete. On the other hand, this is, in a sense, doubting what one sees, or not being certain of what one sees, and really being diverted into a description of one's deficits. However badly one could name them, they represent something that is not awakened, or that the awakening, as it is, is diverted to a description of it. It's rather different than the circumstance that you described as your experience in Movements, yes?

Same Person:
Yes, it was quite different. But I'm not sure I understand what you're saying. I don't feel that I was taken by reaction to it, if that's what you are saying. I even feel now, in myself, this lingering

sense that something is really not quite there. I mean, I am relatively attentive to myself, relatively able to sense what's taking place. I don't feel particularly distant, and yet, there is something palpably missing, which is disturbing, in a way.

Dr. Welch:
I don't mean to put words onto you. I was just trying to follow the tone in which you were putting it, but I think that this is the difficulty that one experiences with much of life. Something's missing. "Is this all it is? Is this it?" is the kind of feeling that one can experience, with a sense of not having a real connection with meaning.

But you seemed to have a connection with meaning in the Movements.

Same Person:
Yes, and I would even say there is a connection with meaning, in a certain way, with this experience tonight, because the meaning, on some level, must be sensed. What I am missing is there somewhere, because I sense it as a lack. And it is not that I feel just out of sorts. I feel very specifically, in a way, because I'm trying to see, that there is something there. I suppose I wish it were more accessible, but I recognize it may not be. And I think that that is a difficult thing for me to be in front of, because it isn't something that I can instantly fix—which is my wish, I suppose.

Dr. Welch:
Which is the one you think you are, perhaps?

Same Person:
Yes.

Dr. Welch:
Then the difficulty is to *stay* with the vision of something empty in an aspect of yourself, yes?

You didn't feel your cup was running over?

Same Person:

No. And on Tuesday, in Movements, it wasn't, again, so much that my cup was running over then either, but there was a solidity about it that makes the contrast clear.

Dr. Welch:

Perhaps "the cup running over" is too easy an analogy, but you were engaged with meaning. You were not engaged with a lack. And more of you was partaking in this. You were moving physically, as well. And there was music that calls in a very special way in the Movements. You would say that, yes?

Same Person:

Yes, I would. And I also wonder about whether the demand called this.

Dr. Welch:

Yes. Well, in both circumstances there was an internal movement with the same, or with a comparable intention, however unarticulated, of being present to yourself. It says something about conditions, doesn't it? And it isn't something that one can, so to speak, *do*, so much as *allow*.

Same Person:

What was said about hiding seems relevant to me, too. It feels like I'm not totally up front with myself right now. Even though I'm being, I think, somewhat honest about what I'm seeing, there is still something that feels a little bit like I'm trying to get away with something. There's something kind of false. It's just in me. It's not like I can do anything about it. That interests me, to see that.

Dr. Welch:

Is that hiding tinged with fear?

Same Person:

Yes.

Dr. Welch:
Fear of what?

Same Person:
I get the impression that it's fear related to being seen as a fraud, somehow.

Dr. Welch:
Being seen as a fraud by oneself, as well as exposing the fact that we all acknowledge and know well, that we are not pure. We're mixed; even at our best, we're mixed. We're not always aware, but sometimes we are aware of that inner acknowledgment of what can be described as the good side and the bad, or the weak or the confused side. Our strength is not "as the strength of ten." At the same time, it's not an acknowledgment that we see clearly, either.

What is fear—as we experience it? I'm not talking about a lion in the street. I'm speaking about this kind of view. Is it something that you can articulate?

Same Person:
Not very easily.

Dr. Welch:
I would venture to say that it is related, somehow, to an anticipation that one will be confronted by something where one does not foresee the presence of enough force, enough energy, to face this anticipated circumstance of a test—that one will be exposed to *oneself*, perhaps. Does that correspond to something that you can sense in your own situation?

Same Person:
Yes. I was just trying to think about this notion of being exposed to myself.

Dr. Welch:
Which, in a way, one has already seen. At the same time, there's

something about—maybe just in the Western world—the tendency to be touched by the habit of guilt, the habit of self-abnegation, instead of being touched by the fragile nature of the human condition, which is not a personal sin, but rather the nature of the unliberated. And what one is seeking is some kind of liberation.

Third Questioner:
Curiously, there's no fear when somehow I feel at home.

Dr. Welch:
That's absolutely right. This is where the joy of freedom is so abundant. There's something about hope and possibility that awakens in that moment of freedom from fear. One doesn't necessarily undertake to come into that state. But when it appears, one knows it well. It's so joyful and so hopeful.

Same Person:
There's an immediate light that enters, and it really seems to come from within. I used to have the impression that everything lit up around me, but I have noticed that, in a way, the darkness inside starts disappearing.

There is also something else connected with this, and that is that there is in me, perhaps all the time, but, at least, at the times I've noticed, an unwillingness to accept help: a sort of pride about it. It takes a certain kind of flexibility, relaxation, and, I guess, what you could call humility—without banging on the drums about it—to say, "I need help."

Dr. Welch:
After all, one has brought one's own inner hero into the circumstance, and to acknowledge that the hero is trembling is not easily seen.

Same Person:
Exactly. And then, of course, what you said, which is that I will not be equal in force to the situation.

Dr. Welch:

This is the characteristic suffering that consists of an internal, threatening, intuition that one hasn't articulated. It doesn't come necessarily as some orderly recognition of something ominous, but rather from a "belly life" and probably from one's earliest experiences with things that appeared to threaten. And it always hits in the guts. It doesn't hit in the cognitive recognition of "It's a good thing not to play fast and loose with a wild wolf."

Same Person:

I'm reminded of an intensive period where I felt as if I were filled to overflowing with the abundance of the vibration. And yet, day after day, there was a gnawing, as it were, at my conscience, that something was missing, something was not right, that I really didn't deserve this, and so on. And I remember one of the people at the head table saying that what was missing was my work. In a way, I thought that was on the mark, because I was coasting, and there was enough protection to cover up the lack of an inner effort. And then, of course, the pendulum swings, and you react against your own laziness, and you begin to chastise yourself, in the wrong way. And that's the other side of that coin.

The thing that is missing, it seems—and I'm not in touch with this all the time—is that I don't work. There is a part of me, perhaps a subconscious part, that kind of knows that. And then there is that immediate reaction when one has a glimpse of it: "What a bad boy." This may date back to the days when I was a child.

Dr. Welch:

The question of "Where are you, Adam?" is still there, isn't it? Adam hasn't yet asked himself that, or recognized what the question was about. God knows, I don't know what the question is about, but I think it's a very interesting situation that God was not asking, "Where are you hiding?" but "Where are you?"—in a circumstance that is characterized by hiding, perhaps. Then what does that then mean about where I am?

First Questioner:
I feel that so much has been given to me in my life, but that it hasn't been received, in a sense, actively. What would active reception be? What is my part? How come I'm not active?

Dr. Welch:
What do you mean by active reception? Have you ever seen, or been present to, or been struck by something that you would call somebody else's active reception? Were you ever shaken by, let's say, something that Mme de Salzmann responded with?

Same Person:
Yes.

Dr. Welch:
When you were struck by a vision that she had of something that you knew perfectly well but had never had that vision of?

Same Person:
Yes, that's true too.

Dr. Welch:
Our best effort at getting near to this is what we could perceive of where she was when one was struck by something that she said— something that one felt had a kind of action—an action *on me.*

Same Person:
I feel it's in relation to just that, something that has an action on me.

Dr. Welch:
Yes. It's a very good question. And it isn't something that one is going to diddle into some kind of an answer. But it does touch something that one has a response to, which is in contrast to what we all experience as our reaction to the demands of life. We used to speak a great deal about action upon me: the effect and the impact of something that had an action on me. It's a very subtle thing to undertake to find words for, but it has a kind of fragrance.

Same Person:
Something has an action on me in a moment, but where am I afterward? It seems very high, but later I feel I am on a different scale from that, and I don't engage myself. And I'm feeling, more and more, that that's what's been lacking. My self, just as I am, needs to be engaged in order for this thing to go on having an action in some way. I don't know. I don't want to get psychological, but...

Dr. Welch:
Well, one thing that I think we can agree about is that experiences of this kind change my level of perception. It changes my scale. And I can hear Mme de Salzmann's voice saying, "But it didn't last." This experience of another scale of perception is not going to persist throughout my day. There is a sharp opening, and everything changes for a moment, and then I'm back where I was. It may be that there are people who are always at that place, but I've never known one who said so. This says something about what is possible in this yearning, this nostalgia, that one has for that sense of aliveness, of opening, of a scale that is nicely labeled "awakening to." But it's not something that can take place, it seems to me, without evoking, in its simplest terms, a kind of attentiveness on a level that I am not usually attending.

It's our question; it's not just your question. One need not feel burdened by how one is—this is something that one has to include. But one sees that one's usual leaden life is not all there is, and that there is a possibility of bringing it to, or having it awakened to, what seems to be another level of perception. One perceives in a way that—it seems not unreasonable to say—is in the direction of something that acts, not something that reacts. It's something that perceives: not doing, but opening.

There are places in oneself to which one sometimes finds it possible to return, where this is a worldview, because it almost becomes a view from a real world—where something requires to be attained. And we're very clumsy at that. We don't know how to stay awake and open, because we are so accustomed to simply dealing with what stirs us—with the telephone that rings, or whatever. Is that the place that we're trying to reach, or is it not?

Same Person:
It's connected.

Dr. Welch:
It seems to me it is.

Same Person:
For example, I've been coming to the group all these years, and yet I've not really known, in some ways, what a group was for. Because there are certain experiences that have been given, that convince, but are so far removed, in a way, from what it is possible to talk about. And then, when I'm talking about something that happened, I'm not in the same state as I was. So why then am I talking? I haven't understood something about the whole idea of the group. I've been thinking about it, and wondering about this, in the sense of engagement, participation.

Dr. Welch:
I don't like to keep quoting the voice of yesterday, but you perhaps remember Mme de Salzmann saying that unless you know *why* you are there, your presence in a group is wasted. What does that mean?

How can you bring this sense of your search for meaning, your wish to be open? And to what? Is this about life and death, or is this just a habit related to something that I say I'm interested in?

Same Person:
It depends. It's been one and it's been the other.

Dr. Welch:
And what then, from that point of view, is the group for? What do you want? What do you wish? What do you need?

Same Person:
Why do we talk about it?

Dr. Welch:
There's something about a consensus that is somehow useful. Is that because one is reassured by seeing there are others who carry the same concern? And does this bring one some sense of maybe being nearer to something that is widely perceived? Or perhaps, instead of being impressionable, one is just suggestible. Which is it?

Same Person:
I haven't come a lot this year, but recently I've been feeling as though one could understand something here that one couldn't understand by oneself, or in a sitting, or in a Movements class.

Dr. Welch:
Understanding is a thing that seems to me to depend on inner conditions. One can understand something in a state of relative awakening, and then the next day, when one is moving to quite another drumbeat, one doesn't even remember what one understood. Isn't that so?

And then one sees that one is divided into at least two sides— maybe more, but at least two. And I look down on the one that is sluggish, and I delight in the one that is more nearly present, and I forget that I can only be whole if I include both. Maybe there are others, but I can love these two. Whether I do or whether I don't, I can certainly not cut one of them off. They appear, and they are both me, and I'm taken by one or the other. I don't see them both at once, and I don't credit one with validity, while the other is a question of yearning. How does one confront this? What is the point of application?

Same Person:
Is it the difference between now and tomorrow morning when the alarm clock goes off?

Dr. Welch:
Well, what one is undertaking to do is to know what *is*, and it has been suggested that the body is more vulnerable, from the point of view of experiencing, than my heart or my head. They take me off, but in my body I can find a place for being. In a way I'm occupying it. I'm with it. I say, "I'm sensing it." It brings me into now. And now. Isn't that so?

In other words, I've got a quandary here, and it has been suggested to me that this is a way in. I don't seem to see the practical reality of this, because it isn't very sensational, and it doesn't last easily, and it taxes my flawed capacity to attend. At the same time, something changes when I'm in touch with the vehicle that is part of my life. I'm more nearly here when I'm not so wholly unaware of all that dispersed physicality. It places me, for a time, in touch with myself in a way that I wasn't a few minutes ago.

And I'm not going to wiseacre about it, but at the same time, whatever it is that I am, I'm more nearly in touch with what I can, in a certain non-distracted way, stay with. And I'm more here than I was. Is that what we've been just trying? It doesn't do more than allow me to experience, for the moment, an aspect of myself in which there are two things. One is what we mean by sensing, and the other, which I didn't actually seek, is a certain quiet, a certain quietude. And it doesn't unspin itself if I wish to share it with somebody who perhaps is trying the same thing.

And this doesn't make me over or answer my questions, but it has a taste of what it is to be present to myself. And I know how difficult it would be if my mind had begun to wander—which it hasn't yet, but I'm sure it will. At the same time, there's a certain continuity of what we could call, at least, a version of a sustained attention. So that, although I don't find this a war of the spirit, still it's much more nearly without a lot of absurd tensions and dreams.

Now, I recognize that this isn't necessarily a way to stay. And, since my concern is articulated as "What to do?" perhaps I should read something and see just how long I can maintain some sense of myself. I can undertake to awaken some associations that I know are possible if I read something that touches on the human situation.

I'm not sure that I could say that this is a connection of the head and the body, but I'm not interested so much in these theories as I am in trying to be present in my head and present in my body. And something moves in me that is another quality of feeling.

Most of these steps, thus far, have been taken with a certain trust, a certain absence of suspicion. In any event, they make sense. This is my small experience of something that I ordinarily ignore for days and weeks at a time. Is this where we are?

Same Person:
Yes.

Dr. Welch:
We can share this, yes?

Same Person:
Yes.

Dr. Welch:
I don't know how one comes to something as big as the implication of action, but the only thing that seems to make sense is to undertake to try to experience oneself in circumstances that one

otherwise misses—not according to the rulebook, and not according to anything except trying to start where there was said to be a "rent in the tent" through which one can get a glimpse of where it is that one wishes to be.

If you hadn't opened this, I wouldn't have benefited from your question. Because, of course, I share your question. These are our questions. One is grateful. So, maybe this is one reason that you're here. Could it be?

Same Person:
Absolutely. But on the receiving end, other people's questions have helped me a great deal over the years.

Dr. Welch:
Where are we? Not just "Where is Adam?" Where are we? Behind the trees? Why are we here?

Second Questioner:
This raises the question of practice. By the grace of God, or by an exchange such as this, I may find myself connected in ways that I ordinarily am not. And yet, it's during everyday life that I'm unwittingly, unknowingly, furthest away from even the question of what the work is, of what it means to work. It's then that I really need a kind of conscience about it. And it raises the question for me that I don't really know how to practice. How do I practice this? This is not something I can obviously manipulate and yet it's necessary to practice—because it's so fleeting.

Dr. Welch:
Well, you know something about this. Not a mistake. Not a bad thing. And it isn't to get good grades. And it isn't to get some result, so much as it is not to miss the trip.

Same Person:
I mean it's pretty obvious what the end of most human life is. It ultimately is a degeneration of human function. It's unquestionable.

So I'm heading toward that end, barring accidents, willy-nilly.

Dr. Welch:
Some of you is.

Same Person:
The ideas that have been expressed in this last exchange do trigger something in my thoughts, but what I noticed was that what really mattered was something that is not perceived by my thinking apparatus. That's what really gave meaning to everything that came about. And because the body is relatively quiescent, I'm not being pulled physically too much.

So, if we're born three-centered beings, why are we so scattered, so one-centered?

Dr. Welch:
A troika can go in three directions at once, apparently. That's where we stand. But there is something about a certain quality of feeling that can appear. A man can call on his head, and he can call on his body, but very often what is required is the engine of what we refer to as emotion. It isn't really the great capacity of the feeling, but it can warm that computation machine between the ears and bring some humanity to it. It is something that distinguishes us from dogs—sometimes, if we're lucky. It's the only real aspect of mankind that Gurdjieff singles out as at the heart of the work: the awakening of conscience, objective conscience, conscience of the level of perception that is perhaps part of the "real world," that awakens one to the real world. It certainly isn't the rather shoddy array of small-time emotional vanity, and considering, and worry, and what he used to call "all this love." [lengthening the vowel in love] This child that is the feeling center, this is the place where one is called to grow up, not just old. Most of us succeed in growing old, without any trouble, sooner or later. Growing up is not so certain.

Lightning Source UK Ltd.
Milton Keynes UK
UKHW040843190123
415622UK00001B/46